A King's Prayer

A Prayer That Touched the Heart of God

by
Jon G. Hoerauf, MA

Cover Photo by Jon Hoerauf

**To order more copies go to
www.lvnfree.com**

Recommendation

My friend, Jon Hoerauf, addresses the reign of King Hezekiah with detailed insight into the stress of a man who desires to live out old covenant instructions faithfully and obediently; yet finds sometimes himself in the throes of Romans 7. Still his reign is more successful than most, because he is determined to live by faith, not by the vicissitudes of his circumstances.

Few people have found the grace of God in an old covenant patriarch as skillfully as Jon has in the life of this king few of us know until we read this profound book. I endorse it to the true seekers of the Word!

Lee LeFebre
President emeritus, Exchanged Life Ministries

Dedication

This book is dedicated to my wonderful wife, Lynn. She has been my friend and companion, and together we have laughed, cried, and grown closer to God. Thank you, Lynn, for everything.

Acknowledgements

I wish to thank the Association of Exchanged Life Ministries, and especially Lee LeFebre of Exchanged Life Ministries in Englewood, CO (www.elmcolo.org). God used Lee to open my eyes to these truths many years ago. It was his teaching and discipleship that laid the foundation for this message.

To contact the Association of Exchanged Life Ministries for teaching, educational resources, discipleship, or counseling, go to http://aelm.org for more information.

Unless otherwise noted, all Bible references are from the New American Standard Bible, 1995 Update.

Table of Contents

Section One
The Foundation

Introduction	10
Chapter 1: Under Siege	12
Chapter 2: A Note About God's Sovereignty	21
Chapter 3: A Family of Royal Dysfunction	26
Chapter 4: A New King – A New Reign	40
Chapter 5: The Setting	46
Chapter 6: The Challenge	61

Section Two
Hezekiah's Prayer

Chapter 7: Hezekiah's Prayer	93
Your Own Prayer	106
Conclusion	117
About the Author	118

Introduction

Ask questions - the more the better. The only problem with asking questions is that sometimes each answer leads to several more questions. That's how it is when you study the Bible. When you open your heart and ask God for insight into His ways, He is more than willing to lead you into deeper understanding of Him. What you will soon discover, however, is that there is no end to this journey as each new path exposes several other journeys of revelation into His glory.

That's where this book came from. It began as a daily Bible reading which raised a few questions and led to cross referencing this same story recorded in other books of the Bible, and then looking into the variations in how the stories were recorded. This search ultimately led to some historical cross references and applications to my own life today. My prayer is that these pages will come alive for you as they did for me and that the Holy Spirit will use them to open your eyes to new avenues for growth and healing.

This is the account of the king of a Middle Eastern nation who lived several thousand years ago, and yet, the struggle is as contemporary as the challenges we face today. Our struggles and temptations really haven't changed that much over the centuries. The comforting thing to remember is that neither has our

God. He still loves us and desires to prove Himself strong on our behalf. God has promised that He is the same "yesterday, today and forever".

Though this is a study on prayer, we will also explore God's character, our motivations, and how one man touched the heart of God.

Enjoy your journey!

Jon Hoerauf

Section One
Under Siege

Chapter 1

To get the most out of this book, it will be helpful to think about a time of castles and fortresses. A time of royal cities surrounded by walls and engulfed in a countryside of small farms. A time that was much different than ours. The clothes, customs, foods, and pastimes were all different from ours. Warfare was also different back then. They used horses rather than heavily equipped SUVs, swords rather than automatic weapons, and spears rather than stealth bombers.

A city's protection was in its walls. Jericho, for example, was said to be an impenetrable city because its walls were so thick that they actually had chariot races on top of them. Rahab, who rescued the spies of Israel after they left Egypt, lowered them down through the window of her home which was actually built into a part of the wall of the city. What this means is that the walls were at least as thick as her house. The thicker your walls, the safer you were. However, a city needs more than walls. For the people of a city to survive, they also need an ongoing supply of food and water.

One of the more effective strategies of war was the siege. When an enemy army marched on an area, the people of the countryside would run to the protection of the walled fortress. From here, the army inside could fight the unprotected enemy from a position of relative safety. That is, as long as their supply of food and water lasted.

That was the genius of a siege. If the attacking army was large enough to completely surround the walls, and if they had enough of their own supplies, they could out last those inside the walls. They would not allow any food to be brought in, and would attempt to block off any water supply entering the city. This process would often take a very long time, but whoever's supplies lasted the longest would win.

As the siege progressed, the army outside would continue to replenish their own supplies by stealing them from the flocks and farms of the surrounding countryside. As they drained the physical resources of those under siege, the enemy would also chip away at their emotional strength. At regular intervals, they would gather near the walls where everyone could hear, and remind the people of how weak they were. They would mock their king and encourage the people to surrender before they died of hunger or thirst.

While the physical pressure was intense, it was the emotional pressure that would become overwhelming. This pressure was not only on the inhabitants of the city, but there was also a tremendous pressure on the king as it was his responsibility to take care of the people. He ultimately faced the choice of surrendering his people into slavery or allowing them to starve to death as free men and women.

We have an example of the burden that this process brings on a city in 2 Kings Chapter 6 where we read about the king of Aram besieging Samaria. During this particular siege, the famine in the city became so intense that the cost of a donkey's head (an unclean animal) was 80 shekels of silver and ½ quart of dove's dung sold for 5 shekels of silver.

A shekel of silver is a measurement which equaled one day's wage. Therefore, during this siege it got so bad that the head of a donkey cost 80 day's wages (at a time when there was no work and therefore no way to get money) and a jar of bird manure cost 5 days wages. Even if you had any money, you would have to be pretty hungry to consider these purchases.

This passage of scripture also records an event of two mothers who made a deal with each other. When one mother didn't want to keep her end of the deal, they went to the king to share their story.

> This woman said to me, "Give me your son that we may eat him today and we will eat my son tomorrow." So we boiled my son and ate him; and I said to her on the next day, "Give your son, that we may eat him"; but she has hidden her son. (2 Kings 6:28-29)

This woman was angry that her friend didn't keep her side of the bargain, but did you catch what that bargain was? The siege and their hunger had driven them mad as they were willing to kill their own children so that they could eat one more meal. Imagine the desperation that these two mothers felt. Being under siege was a terrible thing that created fear, anger, and hopelessness.

How does this apply to us? We will probably never be under siege by an enemy army who is bringing us to a slow, hopeless death, but many of us have experienced similar feelings to those behind the walls. Maybe it is an extended period of unemployment that is draining your hope of ever finding a good job again. Maybe it is a handicapped child and the realization that you will never be able to experience the empty nest that so many others talk about. Maybe it is a disease that you or a loved one can't beat, and no matter how hard you try, your health is still failing. Or maybe it's a breaking, or already broken, relationship that seems to be out of your control to change.

There are many situations in life that may start out simply as unfortunate events. At first, you find a way to deal with them or come up with a new plan to work your way out of it. Your faith is strong and your hopes are high. Maybe you even believe that when this is all over, you will be in a better situation than you are now. The scriptural promises about God's blessings seem very real and, even in the middle of your pain, He seems very close to you.

But time has a way of testing our faith. As the situation continues and the circumstances don't get better, your faith may begin to lose steam. And sometimes, when it has gone on for several months or even years, it begins to feel something like a siege.

You may feel desperately alone and cut off from outside resources. You might be out of new ideas, plans, and proposals. Perhaps you have fasted and prayed in every manner and way that you can think of to get God to act; and He isn't moving. There can come a time when you are completely out of energy to hope anymore. Your mind, your will, and your emotions are drained. You fall asleep at night with a knot in your gut knowing that the morning will only bring more of the same. Eventually, it seems that even if help did come, it would be too little too late. You realize that you are dangerously close to being willing to do anything to make it stop.

Hezekiah, the main character in our story, totally understood these feelings. He, like some of you, lived these feelings in a very real situation. This is a story of his struggle with faith and how he eventually managed to find God amidst all of the other voices calling out for his attention.

Hezekiah was a king, but he was just a person like you and me. He had dreams, hopes, and expectations regarding his life, and he watched as all of those were taken away from him one by one.

My Siege

There was a time in my life when I felt as though I was under siege. One January morning on my way to work, the announcer on the radio said that that particular day was statistically the most depressed day of the year. At the time it struck me as a strange thing to keep track of and I shared it with a few of my colleagues. Later on that afternoon, I felt the statistic personally. I was called into my supervisor's office and informed that I had lost my job. Before the recession hit, I was immediately thrust into the world of unemployment.

I'll never forget the shame I felt a few weeks later as I stood in the kitchen of our local fast food restaurant surrounded by high school kids. As I worked, I remember praying that no one would see me back there; I felt like a total failure. I was a grown man working in a job intended for kids who were saving up for an ipod or maybe their first car. That was quite possibly the hardest job that I have ever had.

After several months of part-time jobs, I decided to go back to school for teaching. At that time, the school atmosphere was ripe for new teachers because there was a large group of experienced teachers who were ready for retirement. I decided to begin the process, and went back to school.

However, after three years of student loans, the economy tanked and no one felt ready to retire. Teachers that had been working for well over 30 years were keeping their jobs in an attempt to ride out the storm. This meant that when a job did happen to open up in my small community, 350 applicants would flood the school with resumes and mine would get lost in the pile. I ended up taking a job as a teacher's aide.

I had prayed fervently for direction, but now found myself more in debt in a sinking economy. I had accumulated over 12 years of college, but was working at a job that only required a High School education. I had been able to interview for a few jobs, but each time I came in second place. By now, I didn't really even expect to get a job. On top of this, because of the economy, I couldn't sell my house to move where there were jobs. I felt stuck.

One night early in December, as the fifth anniversary of losing my job quickly approached, I took my dogs for a walk. The whole experience was closing in on me and I felt as empty as the frigid air that filled my lungs. Five years is a long time to be waiting and hoping on God.

I felt under siege. I had tried everything that I could think of to fix things and I watched in horror as what resources I had slipped away. So this night I decided not to ask God for anything. I decided that as I walked I would use whatever I saw or experienced as inspiration to thank Him.

My first impression was the deadness of everything around me, so I thanked Him that the winters of life don't last forever. I thanked Him that even though all was dark and still, there was life underground just waiting to come out in the spring. It began to snow very lightly, so I thanked God that His blessings were falling down on me like the snow from the sky.

I was reminded of the story in 2 Kings about Elisha. Israel was under attack by the king of Aram, but every time that he planned a surprise attack against Israel, Elisha would warn them. Finally, the king decided that there must be a spy in his camp and he called his men together to find out who it was. One of them told the king what Elisha was doing so the king decided to go capture Elisha.

They went to the city where Elisha was staying and surrounded it during the night. In the morning, Elisha's servant saw the enemy army and basically fell apart. Elisha said, "Do not fear, for those who are with us are more than those who are with them." (2 Kings 6:16)

In this instance, the servant didn't need to depend on his faith, for Elisha prayed a prayer. He asked God to open the servant's eyes. When he did, the servant saw that the mountain was full of horses and chariots of fire completely surrounding the enemy. In other words, Elisha wasn't the one in trouble, the enemy was.

As I thought about this, I remembered that God has promised to keep me in the palm of his hand and protect me so that no one can take me out. That means that if my enemy is surrounding me, he first had to crawl up into God's hand to do it. And, if both my enemy and I are in God's hand, then I am not the one who should be afraid.

I may be surrounded and under siege, but my God is still in charge and all is in His control. As I thanked Him for His protection and provision, it began to snow harder and I remembered comparing the snow to God's blessings falling on me. Even in this time of uncertainty and loss, God seemed to be reminding me that He was right there with me and in total control.

The next morning there was a thick blanket of snow on the ground and I thanked God for His blessings – even the ones that I couldn't yet see.

The Foundation

Chapter 2

A Note About God's Sovereignty

Before we even begin the study of Hezekiah's prayer, we need to consider the topic of the sovereignty of God and how it affects and interacts with our daily life. This is one of the foundational topics of the Christian faith that isn't often considered until life feels out of control and we are looking for answers. Most people have a belief regarding God and His level of influence in the lives of humans, but these beliefs are deeply held and not often considered. It's kind of like your belief in the law of gravity; you know it is there and live your life according to your beliefs about it, but you very seldom find yourself contemplating the affects of gravity on your daily existence with your friends over a café latte.

Many of our beliefs about God are in the same category. We feel strongly about them, but aren't really sure where they came from or why we believe them. When you take the time to examine them closely however, they can move from the area of basic assumptions to strong convictions. A discussion about the topic of prayer often involves the questions of how to successfully communicate our needs to God and why He sometimes doesn't seem to answer when we call. These types of questions are founded in the "Sovereignty of God."

Another time that you come face to face with the sovereignty of God and His influence in the lives of men, is when you consider Israel's history. While God's sovereignty is not the main topic of this book, its importance underlies Hezekiah's journey and therefore will be explored in this study.

Let's face it, we can't understand God's sovereignty any more than we can understand the fact that He has always been here – even before there was someplace called "here" or a concept of time that allows us to use the word "always." He has no beginning, no parents, no inventor; He just is. He has always been an "is." Even though the "isness" of God is not the main point of this book, it is a good representation of the vast gulf between our understanding and the reality of God. Wafting across this gulf is a mysterious mist called the "Sovereignty of God."

The word sovereign has a couple of meanings that give us a look into God's character and being. It can mean the "supreme authority over something," and in this light, we know that God is the supreme authority over all of creation – including the entire spiritual world. God has no equal. It is important to remember that Satan is a created being whose equal would be Michael the archangel, not God. God, alone, is supreme and in a class all of His own.

Sovereign can also mean "having the right to self government." Again, God fits this definition as He alone is self governing. There is no person or power that can tell Him what to do or judge His actions, because He is the one who determines right and wrong.

In some ways it may seem unfair for one being to claim the right to determine truth, justice, and what is right or wrong. When this same being decides that He alone can do whatever He wants and no one has the right to question His actions or motives, we are tempted to cry "foul" and demand a voice in the matter. However, not only is God the sovereign ruler of all things, but He is also pure love and desires only good for us. Truly understanding this makes His rule much easier to accept.

God's sovereignty marks Him as the one who is totally in charge of every aspect of our universe. If you think about it, there is no way for God to be surprised by someone's actions, thoughts or intentions and therefore, He is incapable of making a mistake.

With all of this power and authority as a backdrop, God has mysteriously chosen to include us in His authority and decision making. Somehow, skillfully woven into His sovereignty, is His choice to give us free will.

Upon the canvas of God's ongoing isness and total control, we have been given the responsibility to paint the picture of our choice which becomes the portrait of our life. In a wonderful paradox created within the mind of God, His sovereignty and our free will don't cancel each other out. In fact, they somehow work in unison to bring about His purposes.

God never intended for us to experience pain, fear, or loss and yet He allows us to make the very choices that bring these things into our lives. His allowance of free will is one of His ways of loving us enough to let us go, fully knowing that we might decide to never come back. Love, by its very definition, can't be demanded or required from someone. It must be given freely.

God's love and His willingness to allow us free will, both work together to form who we will become.

We are going to study an Old Testament account of two kings; Sennacherib and Hezekiah. Sennacherib was the king of Assyria, one of Israel's enemies. He was a very powerful and yet self-possessed king who believed that he had created his own destiny. He believed that he had become a great king because he was a great man. He had no place in his belief system for God or His sovereignty. He was the ultimate self-made man.

Hezekiah, on the other hand, was a humble man who knew that his future was in God's hands and therefore turned to Him in his time of desperate need. He was not a perfect man, for he made some pretty bad mistakes. However, he knew enough to turn back to God after his world fell apart, and ask God to take over. Both Sennacherib and Hezekiah had the option to either follow God or live independently of Him, and yet, through their choices and actions, God's will was accomplished.

Chapter 3

A Family of Royal Dysfunction

A time of kings and princes is foreign to us in American society. We are used to a democracy with checks and balances, independent court systems and equal opportunity laws. Our officials are voted in after proving their abilities, and can be voted back out as the people that they serve see fit.

The ancient Jewish kingdom, however, was much different. Men became kings simply because they were born to the right person, then ruled until their death. This meant that if you had a bad king, you might be stuck with him for 20 or 30 years. When the reigning king died, his son would take over. His age, his ability, or his character had nothing to do with it; he became king because it was his destiny.

This made the kings of Judah a very elite club, and Hezekiah was a card holding member. He was only twenty-five years old when he took the throne and enjoyed a twenty-nine year reign in Jerusalem (2 Kings 18:2). Judah had quite a roller coaster ride with leadership throughout her history, but Hezekiah proved to be a refreshing breeze in a hot and dry land.

King David was handpicked by God and became the standard for what a king should be. The Bible often compared individual kings to King David, and unfortunately, too many of them came up short. We are told that Hezekiah, on the other hand, fared very well in this comparison. In fact, he is considered by God to be right up there with David. "He did right in the sight of the Lord, according to all that his father David had done" (2 Kings 18:3).

This is an incredible honor when you realize Hezekiah's family heritage. The family in which a person is raised helps to form their beliefs and attitudes, and Hezekiah came from a rather colorful family. Since the position of being the King of Judah was inherited, all of the previous kings (aside from Saul) were his ancestors. Therefore, the Bible has recorded quite a bit of history regarding Hezekiah's relatives, and as we look at them, we can get a pretty good picture of Hezekiah's family tree.

In the truest sense of the word, all human families have a degree of dysfunction. Some more so than others, but we all have issues. The bigger the issues, the harder it is to break the cycle. A person is a combination of their own makeup plus the makeup of their family habits and traditions. So to truly understand Hezekiah's life, we need to understand his family history.

Israel's first king was Saul, and though he was not an ancestor of Hezekiah, he did set precedence for what it meant to be a king in Israel. When you examine his failures as a king, you can see a pattern begin to develop. He built his kingdom while depending on his own abilities and decisions rather than trusting God. For example, Saul tried to do the right thing in the wrong way when he became impatient while waiting for the prophet Samuel.

At one point in time, Samuel told Saul to wait for seven days before going to war, and at the end of those seven days Samuel would meet him and make a sacrifice to the LORD. On the morning of the seventh day Saul began to get nervous and by that evening, he couldn't take the pressure anymore. He knew that he needed God's blessing if he was going to win the battle, so he decided to take matters into his own hands rather than wait for Samuel. Saul decided that he would carry out the sacrifice without Samuel.

He quickly found out that good motives are no excuse for operating independently of God, because as soon as he was done, Samuel showed up. As Samuel chastised Saul he told him, "to obey is better than sacrifice" (1 Sam. 15:22). In other words, living in union *with* God is much more important than simply doing the right things *for* God.

Something similar happened closer to home for Hezekiah with his great-grandfather Uzziah, who had his own problems with following God. He actually started out his reign by following and honoring the Lord in what he did, becoming very powerful in the process. However, as so often happens, as he grew powerful he also became proud.

In an act of disregard to God's law, he entered the temple of the LORD and burned incense on the altar. This was a privilege reserved for the priests, and when they confronted him, Uzziah became angry with them for daring to question him. Because of his arrogance, the LORD immediately struck him with leprosy and he lived the rest of his life cut off from the house of the LORD. This may sound harsh, but God wants us to understand our total dependence upon Him. When we understand and acknowledge our limitations, we can enjoy His strength.

So, how did Hezekiah do in the area of dependence upon God? The first thing that any political ruler does once he takes office gives us a good picture of what he considers to be vital; Hezekiah is no exception.

The very first thing that Scriptures record him doing after he took office is re-opening the temple and repairing it. The temple had been so shamelessly abused by past kings that it needed to be repaired and cleansed before worship could be reinstituted. Hezekiah called on the priests, those set aside by the LORD to work in the temple, to come into it and purify it.

It is significant that he did not try to do this work himself, but used the lines of authority and duty that God had set up. His great-grandfather, Uzziah, had paid dearly for making a mistake in this area. Hezekiah seemed to have a handle on this lesson because he put these important temple duties in the hands of the priests and Levites instead of taking the honor for himself.

Hezekiah's actions give us a glimpse into the character of this young king. True character, however, is revealed under pressure and deepens over time. God was pleased, but as we will see, He desired to take Hezekiah even deeper in his dependence on Him. Hezekiah's spiritual growth was not yet complete.

Dependence Upon & Union With the LORD

Let's step aside from our story for a moment to discuss another vital topic; total dependence upon and union with God. This is a major theme throughout the Bible and a vital aspect of our Christian walk. Human beings by nature are weak - at least compared to God. We need food, water, air and sleep. If we try to go for very long without any one of these, we will begin to fall apart.

Let's say for a moment that I came up behind you, put my hand over your mouth and nose, and blocked your air. You have a strong need for air, so it is unlikely that you would simply think, "Well, in 3 or 4 minutes I will probably pass out and after around 12 minutes I will be dead." No, chances are you would fight me to get your air back. Even if I were built like someone who had trained for a cage fight, you would do whatever you could to get my hand away. In fact, the longer that you went without air, the harder you would fight me and the more tactics you would use to get your need for air met.

Along with physical needs, we also have emotional, relational, and spiritual needs. The longer these needs go unmet, the harder we tend to try to find a way to get them met. When life gets overwhelming we become stressed, and when we get stressed, our minds don't work as well and we can make poor decisions. This leads to more stress, and can eventually lead to complete emotional or physical breakdown.

The problem is that we don't want to admit, or may not recognize it, but we are weak. As humans, we are tempted to believe that if we would try hard enough, and if we were given enough time, then we could accomplish anything.

This, however, is simply not true. God created us with needs. No matter how strong or self-sufficient you may be, you still have needs. Foremost of these, is a need for intimacy and fellowship with Him. It seems that when we begin to feel independent and strong in ourselves, we become isolated - especially from Him. Sometimes, we isolate ourselves because we feel weak, but in our weakness or our strength, we are meant to live in union with God.

To look into God's face is to experience our smallness, and since being small may be threatening to us, this can be quite unnerving. However, when we are at peace in God's fatherly love for us, being small can be very comforting. When we realize that He is in control, it makes it safe for us to be out of control. When we realize that He knows the future, it becomes OK that we don't.

This whole idea poses a real problem for most people. Humans tend to spend a great deal of their time being strong, capable, and independent. However, we function best as humans when we remember that God is the Creator and we are the created ones. He is the Father and we are His children. He is the source of strength and we are the vessels that His strength flows through.

Understanding that God is supreme is comforting when you know how much He loves you. He loves you so much that He was willing to give up His very life so that you could become His child and experience that life. God is supreme because He is God. What He desires is to become supreme in every single area of your life.

For God to be supreme in our lives we need to come to the point of being willing to follow Him even when it doesn't make sense to us. We need to develop total trust in Him and His character. This is a process of becoming aware of God's love and provision for us, rather than seeing Him as someone with a desire to keep us down. When the world is on your shoulders and you have no one to lean on but yourself, life is difficult - life is impossible. But, when you allow Him to take your burdens and give you His resources, you have the room you need to live life as it comes.

As we see from Samuel's response to Saul when he told him that to obey is better than sacrifice, God is more interested in our relationship *with* Him than with us performing a particular duty *for* Him. When we act presumptuously and take matters into our own hands, we are demonstrating our belief that we know how to run things better than God. Basically, we find true peace and joy as we live our life totally dependent on God and in intimate union with Him.

Hezekiah found himself in a very bad situation. Part of it was his own fault and part of it was his circumstances, but he knew that he could count on God and he wasn't alone. Like Hezekiah, we may not enjoy our circumstances, but these circumstances may be the very thing that will be used to propel us into greater levels of victory.

Hezekiah's Father

When the priests and Levites entered the Temple to carry out Hezekiah's cleansing, they found a disgusting trail left by the previous kings. This trail led right up to and included Hezekiah's father, Ahaz. Scripture says of Ahaz that, "he did not do what was right in the sight of the LORD his God, as his father David had done" (2 Kings 16:2, emphasis added).

Ahaz was a very evil man. He made molten images for the Baals, burned incense to false gods, consulted mediums and spiritists, and worshipped false gods on the "high places."

These "high places" were usually up on a hill and were set aside for cult worship. Often the scriptures refer to them in conjunction with the worship of the Baals and Asherah (the god and goddess of fertility). Their worship included sexual immorality to excessive degrees in the hopes of bringing fertility to the crops, animals and people. Ahaz, we are told, made it a common practice to "worship" on these high places.

Another testimony of the depravity of Ahaz was expressed while he was in Damascus where he saw a certain kind of altar that he liked. He had one built just like it and actually used it to replace the one that Solomon had put in the Temple.

Eventually, he closed the Temple completely, stripped it of its holy things and openly worshipped the gods of Damascus. Ahaz even went so far as to sacrifice his own sons in fire. In his actions he copied, "the abominations of the nations whom the Lord had driven out before the sons of Israel" (2 Chron. 28:3).

In the Hebrew culture someone's name meant a great deal. It tended to be a phrase or a short sentence that comprised a blessing or a promise about God. This way, every time the person would hear their name, this blessing would be spoken over them. It is interesting to note that the name "Ahaz" literally means, "Yahweh holds him fast." By giving him this name at his birth, his parents were speaking a blessing over him. Tragically, Ahaz did not live up to his name.

What's in a Name?

Not only were the names of people significant, but the various names ascribed to God also hold great meaning. Knowing the literal translation for these names can give us a much deeper understanding of God, His character, and His promises.

One thing worth noting in regard to God's name is the word "LORD" spelled with all capital letters (sometimes translated as Jehovah). This is the way our English Bible translates YHWH - God's personal name. When Moses was sent by God from the burning bush into Egypt, he asked God to tell him His name. As mentioned above, in the Hebrew culture someone's name meant a great deal. People's names were often phrases or even full sentences which were carefully chosen for them. An example closer to home would be the names of many Native Americans such as "Sitting Bull" or "Dances with wolves."

There are several examples in the Bible of God changing someone's name to show that He had changed the person (i.e. Abram to Abraham or Jacob to Israel). The meaning in their new name was the evidence of a deeper truth which He had developed within the person. When Moses asked God what His name was, he was actually asking God to reveal Himself. He was saying in effect, "Who are You God?" "You are asking me to do an incredibly hard thing and I need to know more about You first."

To totally put God's character into something which we can understand is an impossible task, and to ask Him to narrow it down to one sentence is almost ridiculous. However, God did just that in a very beautiful and meaningful way. He told Moses that His name is YHWH or "I AM." What does God mean by this?

Partially, it means that God is always present, everywhere and to everyone. In other words, He is totally present with you right now, which means that His mind isn't wandering off to something that happened last week or something that will happen tomorrow. If you are talking with someone and that person is looking into your eyes and hanging on every word you speak, you could say that he is "totally present" to you.

As humans, we can only be "present" to one thing at a time. However, God is totally present to each of us at all times. He is actually totally present to every object in the universe and intimately involved in keeping everything working. God, who is the sovereign ruler of the universe, is tirelessly tending to you as if you were His prize rose bush. He trims your dead leaves, waters you and exposes you to the right amount of sunshine and rain. He never turns His back or walks away because you are His.

"I AM" also means that not only is He here in this present moment, but He is already in tomorrow morning waiting to greet you when you wake up. To God, all things and times are present all at once. He is. As created beings, we are bound to time and space and therefore see things as past, present, or future. God is uncreated and therefore greater than time and space. He experiences all things as present and is present for all things. The fact that this is incomprehensible to us only goes toward the proof that God is totally "other" than we are.

The Old Testament gives us further understanding as to what God was saying when He called Himself "I AM." He would often reveal Himself in a particular way to meet the need of a certain person at that specific time. This would involve a new name that was often introduced as "I am the LORD your…"

When He appeared to Abram to announce the birth of Isaac He said, "I am God Almighty" (El Shaddai – Genesis 17:1). He was revealing to Abram that He can do all things - even give a son to a very old couple. At one point God promised to protect the Israelites from the diseases which He put on the Egyptians. Along with this promise, He revealed another name for Himself when He said, "I, the LORD, am your healer" (Jehovah Rapha – Exodus 15:26).

Some other names that God used to describe His character are:

Jehovah Sabbath – Lord of Hosts
Jehovah Jireh – The Lord our Provider
Jehovah Nissi – The Lord our Banner or Victory
Jehovah Tsidkenu – The Lord our Righteousness
Jehovah Rohi – The Lord our Shepherd
Jehovah Shalom – The Lord our Peace

Moses was asking God to tell him who He was and probably expecting a convincing explanation. However, God cannot be known in an instant, but He reveals Himself over a lifetime as He becomes all that we need.

When Moses asked, God said that His name is "I AM." In other words He was saying, "I AM what you need in this instant." Do you need protection? Then, I AM your protection. Do you need healing? Then, I AM your healing. Do you need a shepherd? Then, I AM your shepherd.

God desires to reveal Himself as He becomes for you all that you need Him to be in each moment of life. This is the Christian walk; getting to know God in an increasingly deeper and more personal way as you call on Him to meet your needs. This method also fits with God's desire to reveal to us our total dependence on Him. While we may desire to have the whole picture all at once, it is only through a daily and ever deepening revelation of Him that we can truly get to know Him.

As we will see, Hezekiah had a real and present need, and all of this was wrapped up in the name, the "LORD our God" (2 Kings 19:19). As you read through the scriptures, look for times when lord is written as "LORD" and discover a new name for God and then apply it to your personal needs.

Chapter 4

A New King - A New Reign

The Passover Reinstated

Hezekiah did not follow his father's lead; instead he began a series of reforms that brought Jerusalem back to God. Foremost of these reforms was the reinstitution of the Passover.

The Passover was the festival meal that celebrated the LORD passing over Israel when He killed the first born of Egypt in His tenth and final plague against the Pharaoh. The importance that God put on the Passover is reflected in the fact that when He instituted it, He reordered the Hebrew calendar making that month the first month in their year. It is a festival which demonstrated many rich truths concerning God's love, grace, protection and provision for his people, while pointing to the coming of Jesus and His ultimate sacrifice. When God first instituted the Passover, He said that the Jews should, "observe this event as an ordinance for (them) and (their) children forever" (Ex. 12:24). Unfortunately, throughout their history, the Jews often ignored this celebration as they turned to other gods.

When the Passover was celebrated, the Jews were reminded of their covenant with the LORD and their attention was drawn back to Him. It was one of only three festivals in which all Jews were to travel to Jerusalem to celebrate. This is why Hezekiah made an appeal throughout the land for everyone to come to Jerusalem to celebrate the Passover, "for they had not celebrated it in great numbers as it was prescribed" (2 Chron. 30:5). Hezekiah urged the people to return to, "The LORD (their) God so that His burning anger may turn away from (them)" (2 Chron. 30:8). However, when the messengers gave this appeal to the people of Judah, most of the people, "laughed them to scorn and mocked them" (2 Chron. 30:10).

Imagine Hezekiah's feelings as he heard this. He was attempting to change the direction of his nation and instead of following him, they mocked him. As a new ruler, it would have been very important for him to set a precedence that he is now in charge and the people were obligated to follow his rule. However, when the people not only refused to come to Jerusalem, but even mocked his attempts to rally them, he must have felt defeated and even intimidated. He may have been tempted to give up on the reforms and leave the people to themselves, or possibly even go along with them to gain their popularity. Remember, he was only 29 years old and didn't have a good example to follow.

However, he was not distracted by their response and decided to go forward with his celebration in spite of them. His Passover celebration didn't fail. In fact, it was so successful that the whole group who did celebrate with Hezekiah decided to continue for a second seven days of praise and worship.

This is even more amazing when you remember the sacrifice that the people were making to be there. They had to leave their homes and travel to Jerusalem. Not only did they have to pay their own expenses, but they were not able to work during that time. Along with that, they were probably seen as "Yahweh freaks" by their neighbors who had mocked Hezekiah for his idea. By celebrating the Passover they were choosing to trust that God would provide for them as they were obedient to His word. This is exactly what God was looking for when He instituted the Passover in the first place.

Any time that God's people genuinely worship Him, His power is released into their lives, and this was no exception. The passion of the Passover celebration continued as all who were present went back out into the cities of Judah and removed the high places and tore down the sacred pillars where Ahaz had worshiped. Along with this, Hezekiah commanded those in Jerusalem to "give the portion due to the priests and Levites so that they might devote themselves to the law of the LORD" (2 Chron. 31:4). Hezekiah's enthusiasm was so infectious that the people responded in abundance and fully supplied for the needs of the priests and Levites.

Further Reforms by Hezekiah

Judah had become so degenerated by the time that Hezekiah became king that they even worshipped the bronze serpent that God had ordered Moses to make in the desert. It is incredible to realize the implications of this act of idolatry.

After the Lord freed Israel from Egypt and introduced them to the Promised Land, a land given freely to them to possess, they turned on God and complained. While it may not seem so serious to complain, what they were actually doing was telling God that He was a fool for bringing them out of Egypt and if He would only leave them alone they would have fared much better.

It was God's desire that they understand their total dependence on Him because He knew that this was necessary before they could ever be truly free. To accomplish this, He sent serpents to bite the Israelites, and those who were bitten died from the poison. When they realized their foolishness and understood that God was really the one in charge, He instructed Moses to make a bronze serpent and raise it up on a pole. Whoever looked at it would be healed.

This was a beautiful picture of God's grace and a powerful foreshadowing of Jesus as He was raised up on a cross for our salvation from death into life. Imagine how the newly formed and polished bronze glistened in the bright desert sun. You could see it all over the camp. In the same way, Jesus on the cross still shines throughout history and attracts the attention of a broken and dying world.

By Hezekiah's time, this symbol had become a false god that the descendants of those in the wilderness actually worshipped. Once again, what God had intended to be used to lead people to Himself had been turned into a symbol of rebellion and independence from Him. When Hezekiah became king, he honored God by destroying this serpent and showing that the Creator is more important than what He creates.

Again, when you consider the political implications of such an action you get a better feeling for the commitment that Hezekiah demonstrated by doing this. For him to destroy the actual serpent that Moses had fashioned with his own hands was something like the President of the United States destroying the Declaration of Independence or the Liberty Bell. This serpent was a national treasure that could never be replaced and its destruction could have definitely brought a strong resistance. A king is only as strong as his following, and Hezekiah was taking a great risk by going in this "new" direction. However, he chose God's blessing over the popular vote and prospered because of it.

Hezekiah did such a thorough job of reforming Judah that the Bible says that he, "trusted in the LORD the God of Israel; so that after him there was none like him among all the kings of Judah, nor among those who were before him" (2 Kings 18:5). We are told that the reason this is true is that he, "clung to the LORD; he did not depart from following Him, but kept His commandments" (2 Kings 18:6). To "cling to" in the Hebrew language means to cleave, to follow hard, to stick to, abide or to pursue.

Hezekiah loved the LORD in such a fervent way that this relationship was described as him pursuing or sticking to the LORD. As a result of this fervency for the LORD, the Bible states that, "the LORD was with him; wherever he went he prospered" (2 Kings 18:7).

In spite of his past, in spite of the pressures of those around him and in spite of his youth, Hezekiah clung to the LORD and stood firm. It is from this secure foundation that he took on the challenge of being king.

Chapter 5

The Setting

Hezekiah, the man of God, has purified Judah from within by destroying the sources of idol worship and, as the representative of the nation, has turned his focus totally toward God. Now, as the stage is set, the drama begins. By destroying the peoples' gods consisting of stone, wood and bronze he conquered the enemies of God. The question now is, "how will he do when these spiritual forces come at him in the flesh?"

By this time in history, Israel and Judah had separated into two nations and they were often at war with each other. However, no matter how they felt about each other, geographically they were close together and therefore what happened to one could usually be expected by the other. In Hezekiah's fourth year as king something happened to his cousins and we can assume that he watched closely. In this early part of his reign, the young king watched as the mighty and experienced king of Assyria besieged Israel.

A siege is a terrible thing to endure, and even the threat of a siege of this magnitude would bring fear to a city. The longer that a siege lasted, the more desperate the people within the city would become. Eventually, rational thinking would give way to fear and once their hearts melted, the battle was all but over.

Effective warfare is as much psychological as it is brute force. Whether you are fighting a war or playing basketball, much of the victory is attributed to the "mind games" that you play.

The Assyrians were notorious for being cruel to those that they took into captivity. They would line them up, pierce their nose or lip (two extremely sensitive areas) with a hook, and put a chain through the hook. They would then chain a long line of people together and march them off to captivity. As they became famous for this cruelty, just the thought of Assyria coming to attack your fortress could bring the strongest warrior to his knees.

Add to this the dwindling supply of food and water and combine it with the psychological badgering, and pretty soon fears mounted and hope began to fade. With time, all hope was exhausted, desperation set in and frustration took over. With the threat of starvation and torture looming, and the rumors of impending doom circulating, the fears of the people would turn to anger. Ultimately, this anger would be directed at their king. People will do almost anything under these circumstances and even the most loyal will eventually give themselves willingly into slavery to avoid torture or a painful death.

This is the place where Hezekiah finds himself. By the time Sennacherib came to Hezekiah, God had already used the king of Assyria to take Israel away into exile for not obeying Him (2 Kings 18:11-12). Israel was under siege for three very long years before they finally broke under the pressure of the Assyrians. This was three years for Hezekiah to watch the Assyrians at a close range and to have the images of this siege burned into his memory.

When we ponder images of defeat, they take root and produce a deep fear.

Hezekiah Stands Firm

"And the LORD was with him; wherever he went he prospered. And he rebelled against the king of Assyria and did not serve him" (2 Kings 18:7). The Hebrew word "prosper" as used in this verse refers to the idea of having insight or wisdom. In other words, because Hezekiah clung to the LORD he had wisdom and insight in all that he did. We read that he, "trusted in the LORD" (2 Kings 18:5) which in Hebrew means that he felt safe and literally "careless" in the LORD.

We often think of "careless" as a negative word, and it can be if you are thinking of being reckless or uncaring toward other people. When we are told to cast all of our cares on God, however, the word "careless" has a different connotation. We may think of it as being care-free or free of all cares.

Hezekiah seemed to become "care-less" in God's covenant love and protection. He realized that he was not under the authority of a pagan king but of a Holy God. This understanding of God's love and protection can give a supernatural boldness to step out into whatever He brings our way.

Back in Exodus, as God was preparing the Israelites to enter the land of Canaan, He told them, "you shall not worship their gods, or serve them, or do according to their deeds; but you shall utterly overthrow them, and break their sacred pillars in pieces" (Exodus 23:24). Hezekiah took this command to heart and decided to live accordingly.

While Israel was under siege, and for 7 years after they fell to the Assyrians, Hezekiah remembered God's promises. He rebelled against the king of Assyria by not paying tribute to him or serving him in any way. He even demonstrated his freedom by going to war against the Philistines and defeating them during this time.

The Enemy Returns - Hezekiah Stumbles

However, 10 years after Assyria began their siege on Israel, they again turn their attention to Jerusalem and Hezekiah. Ten years is a very long time, and it appears that it affected Hezekiah's boldness. The bold carelessness which he exhibited over 10 years earlier seems to have faded and grown cold. When

Sennacherib came up against the fortified cities of Jerusalem, Hezekiah basically fell apart.

Can you imagine the mental pictures that played across the screen in his mind or the tragic scenarios that flooded his imagination? Maybe you have experienced a promise of God that at first seemed so real and exciting, but as time wore on, you became worn down. Time has a way of etching away at our strength, our dedication, and our energy.

It seems that Hezekiah forgot God's promises, got scared of Sennacherib, and apologized to him for his former rebellion. He then told Sennacherib, "I have done wrong. Withdraw from me; whatever you impose on me I will bear" (2 Kings 18:14).

Sennacherib demanded that Hezekiah give him the equivalent of 22,680 lbs. of silver and 2,268 lbs. of gold. Hezekiah took all the silver from his own treasuries and, when that wasn't enough, he turned to God's temple for the rest. He still needed more so he went as far as to cut off the gold from the doors of the temple.

This act is a good example of misplaced fear. Hezekiah was actually willing to steal from and mutilate the temple of the LORD in order to please another human being. It is amazing what our fears can do to us when we allow them to take over.

It's also interesting to note that Hezekiah's father had done the same thing to appease the king of Assyria years earlier. There are numerous examples in scriptures where a son repeated the very sins of his father. This demonstrates a common truth. Unless we are aware of our weaknesses and actively pursue God's healing, we will often repeat the sins of our ancestors.

When the heat was on, Hezekiah turned to his own resources and the best that he could humanly do to solve his problem. This hadn't worked for his father, and it didn't work for him. In looking at a similar account in the life of Hezekiah's father, Ahaz, we read, "Although Ahaz took a portion out of the house of the LORD and out of the palace of the king and of the princes, and gave it to the king of Assyria, it did not help him" (2 Chron. 28:21).

Sennacherib, like any other bully, was not satisfied with his pay off and sent his army to besiege Jerusalem anyway. Hezekiah would be forced by circumstances which were too great for him to turn back to the LORD.

These few chapters give us a good chance to watch the spiritual growth of Hezekiah. Early in his reign he tackled national traditions and his family ways. As discussed earlier, he came from what we would consider a very dysfunctional family that had built fortresses of belief systems in his mind. He successfully tore down these belief systems by continually reminding himself of the truth about God. Now he is facing a new challenge with an enemy in the physical and psychological realm.

We need to remember that nothing can come our way that has not been allowed by God. When He allows an attack to come our way, He also provides us with what we need to overcome; and in this situation He again proves Himself faithful.

Hezekiah learns an expensive lesson as this test begins, but as we will see, he turns back to God and begins a new chapter in his spiritual walk. Again, God meets him in grace, and in His forgiveness a new level of power is released through Hezekiah.

Hezekiah's Encouragement

Something has changed in Hezekiah. This same account is recorded in three different places in the Bible - (2 Kings 18-19, 2 Chronicles 29-32 and Isaiah 36-37). It's difficult to tell for sure from the texts, but it appears that after Hezekiah paid off the king of Assyria out of fear, he changed his attitude. Possibly because the king of Assyria accepted the payoff which Hezekiah gave him, but then attacked Judah anyway. Another possibility is that he felt convicted for his sin and realized that he didn't want to follow his father's path of independence from God. Hezekiah, you will remember, knew God personally and had experienced the reality of trusting Him fully. Once a person has experienced this intimacy with God, everything else pales in comparison.

Whatever the reason, Hezekiah assembled the military officers and encouraged them by saying,

> Be strong and courageous, do not fear or be dismayed because of the king of Assyria, nor because of all the multitude which is with him; for the One with us is greater than the one with him. With him is only an arm of flesh, but with us is the LORD our God to help us and to fight our battles. (2 Chron. 32:7-8)

With these few words of encouragement Hezekiah was speaking volumes, both to the troops and about himself.

Knowing the historical background in which this took place gives us a much deeper understanding of what is going on. One of the Biblical commands that God gave concerning the king was that as soon as he took the throne he must write out, by hand, his own personal copy of the first five books of the Bible (the whole Bible at that time). He was to keep it with him at all times and read it continually. This would keep God's commands and promises in the forefront of the king's mind. As the ruler of the nation, the king was the one responsible for the spiritual direction of the people, and God knew that the best way for him to carry out his political duties was to be spiritually mature and growing.

The same principle holds true for us today. To be prepared for the daily battle with the Devil, the world, and our own flesh, we need to follow the same principle which God gave to the kings. God's truths need to be second nature and always in our conscious mind so that they can be drawn upon whenever needed. This is accomplished through repetition and practice as a person continually "sets his mind", or chooses to think on truth (Col. 3:2).

By reading the words that Hezekiah said to his men, we can be sure that he had been memorizing and encouraging himself with God's word. Compare what Hezekiah said with what Moses told Joshua. "Be strong and courageous, do not be afraid or tremble at them, for the LORD your God is the one who goes with you. He will not fail you or forsake you" (Deut. 31:6).

Hezekiah is not just making this up as he goes along; he is simply being obedient to God's commands and quoting scripture to his troops. He is acknowledging that this very real and physical situation has a spiritual answer.

Hezekiah is remembering someone else's spiritual victory and applying the same principle to his own, very personal situation. These words were spoken by Moses long before Hezekiah was born, but he still chooses to believe that they apply directly to his life and his situation.

Sometimes we might see the Bible as a history book that doesn't necessarily apply to us today. We need to remember that, for Hezekiah, the section of scripture that we are studying hadn't been written yet, and God was revealing Himself moment by moment. Long after Hezekiah died, God said, "For I the LORD, do not change" (Malachi 3:6). Life may change, people may think that the world has become more contemporary, but God is the same and His principles for victory never change.

God's Battle Plan

Chapter 20 of Deuteronomy gives the plans which the Israelites were to follow when they went into battle. God tells them how to respond when they go out for battle and their eyes see the great number of men on the opposing side causing their emotions to go haywire. He also told them that the enemy will have horses and chariots which were the armaments of only the rich and more modern nations.

When Moses spoke these words, Israel had just left 400 years of slavery. Fighting experience and strategy of war was not a part of their history. It may be easier to understand if one pictures a tribe of Australian Aborigines armed with spears and wooden arrows looking down the barrel of the United Nations and their stealth bombers.

God told them that when they find themselves in this situation that they should not be afraid of their enemies for these weapons are nothing when compared to God's strength and resources. These words, however, are not simply meant to encourage them back at camp on the night before the big battle. Deut. 20:2 tells us that the priest is to remind them of this *when they are approaching the battle.* This means that they are almost face to face with the enemy, fully dressed for battle and on the verge of erupting into life or death warfare.

It would appear from an earthly standpoint that this is not the time for a spiritual rally, an old-time tent meeting, or a Bible study. While they are standing there, on the verge of what would seem to be certain annihilation, it seems a bit late for encouragement. Also, if there was any encouragement to bring, you would think that it should come from their general who had fought and defeated many enemies of his own. However, it is not the military leader who is to address the soldiers, it is the spiritual leader.

While they are standing face to face with a very physical enemy, much stronger and better equipped than them, they are to wait patiently for the priest to make his way to the front of the line so that he can address the troops. At the height of what would otherwise seem to be a military procedure, God reveals that it is actually a spiritual one.

What is the priest to say at this threshold of certain annihilation? Part of what he is to tell them is not to be afraid because, "the LORD (their) God is the one who goes with (them), to fight for (them) against (their) enemies" (Deut. 20:4). Earlier we listened in as Hezekiah said, "for the one with us is greater than the one with him…with us is the LORD our God to help us and to fight our battles." Hezekiah is quoting scripture to his troops! He is approaching a very physical problem with spiritual weapons.

Again, there are significant real life applications for the Christian. Paul tells us,

> Our struggle is not against flesh and blood, but against the rulers, against the powers, against the world forces of this darkness, against the spiritual forces of wickedness in the heavenly places. (Eph. 6:12)

It is very easy to look around with physical eyes and perceive our problems in merely the physical realm, when in reality we live in a very spiritual world. If our problems consisted merely of the physical realities around us, then Jesus would have told us that a superior intellect, muscular strength or a quick wit would set us free. What He did say is, "the truth will set you free" (John 8:32). What God reveals as truth *is* truth - even if it counters human logic and what our five senses reveal.

This principle of turning your attention away from the source of your fears and toward God still holds true today. You may not face the same physical enemies today that they faced in the Bible, but your enemies are just as real. Sickness, unemployment, relational problems...whatever it is that is causing your knees to buckle in fear, must still bow in the presence of the almighty God who has promised to bless and keep you. The answer to fear is a deeper knowledge of God's love for you.

Moses introduced a blessing to the Israelites that we still use today. He said,

> The LORD bless you, and keep you; the LORD make His face shine on you, and be gracious to you; the LORD lift up His countenance on you, and give you peace. (Numbers 6:24-26)

This is an amazing blessing that not only spoke to the Israelites, but speaks directly to us today.

The word "bless" actually means "to kneel" and brings the idea of honoring someone. The word "keep" means to "guard, protect or treasure up." In the early days of castles, the keep was a strong tower where the royal family could be safe while a war was being fought outside.

The idea of "lifting up His countenance" has to do with acknowledging you as special or precious to him. Suppose that you and I are old friends who haven't seen each other for several years. There just so happens to be a time when I am speaking to a large audience in your city and I know that you are going to be there. As I scan the crowd I am looking at several people, but when I finally see you, my eyes light up as I smile and nod. This is the picture meant here by God lifting up His countenance on you. He is searching over the whole human race looking for you, and when He finds you, His eyes light up and He smiles because you are precious to Him.

Finally, the word "peace" is Shalom. This is also very rich word that means much more than peace. It comes from a word that means "to be in a covenant of peace" or "to be complete." It brings with it the idea of being at peace within, even though there is no peace in your external surroundings. It is similar to the idea brought up in the New Testament of peace beyond human understanding.

So, when you think of it in this way, it's like saying,

> May the Almighty God, who is in a blood covenant with you, publicly honor you in front of your enemies; may He keep you as safe and protected as His most valuable treasures that are stored in His vault; may His eyes sparkle with joy and anticipation

every time He looks your way; and may you experience peace as only He knows it.

Remembering your value in God's eyes allows you to draw your attention to Him rather than toward your problems. You matter to Him and He has every intention of being there with you and for you.

Chapter 6

The Challenge

The Anatomy of Temptation

Sennacherib, the king of Assyria, sent three of his servants to Jerusalem with a message for King Hezekiah. They came to the wall of Jerusalem and called out to the king, so Hezekiah sent out his servants to receive their message. The servants of Sennacherib began with accusing questions about Hezekiah's audacity to stand against the king of Assyria. They then moved through a series of stages of psychological warfare with the intent of wearing down the people of Jerusalem.

As we look at this section verse by verse, we will notice the close parallels to the way Satan works as he tempts a Christian to doubt God and His provision. This doubt leads a person to take his eyes off of God and put them on himself in an attempt to meet his own needs - this is the heart of sin.

How can the enemy get away with this? Every Christian knows that God is far better equipped to meet his needs than he is by himself. Why is it that someone with a new spirit, which is now united with the Holy Spirit, still chooses to rely on his own resources (the flesh) instead of trusting in God? The enemy of our soul uses deception to turn our eyes away from God and toward our fears.

Satan has been deceiving people since the beginning of time and, by looking at Hezekiah's temptation, we can learn something for our own life. The temptation develops and progresses through several stages that mirror temptations that we face today.

For this section, we will be exploring 2 Kings 18:18-37. It would be very helpful to open your Bible to these verses and read through them before continuing.

1. Boldness

The first thing that we notice is the boldness and confidence which is used by the servants of the king of Assyria. When someone speaks boldly and refuses to back down from his position, even if he is wrong, he can wear down your trust in your own thinking. If this person can keep up this bold front for a long enough time, you may begin to believe that he is right. This is the first tactic which the enemy used against Hezekiah.

When the army came to Jerusalem, they yelled out, "Say now to Hezekiah, 'Thus says the great king, the king of Assyria, what is this confidence you have?" (2 Kings 18:19) You will notice that they referred to

Sennacherib not simply as another king, but they called him, "the great king, the king of Assyria." By simply mentioning Assyria they brought in all of the fear attached with that Kingdom. Along with this, they called Sennacherib the "great king" which brought in the assumption that he was somehow a king above all other kings.

2. Indirect attack on God

With this boldness, they planted a seed of doubt into Hezekiah's mind by challenging and attempting to undermine his confidence. They are attacking his confidence on both the physical and spiritual fronts. First, the spokesman says,

> "You say (but they are only empty words), 'I have counsel and strength for the war.' Now on whom do you rely, that you have rebelled against me? Now behold, you rely on the staff of this crushed reed, even on Egypt; on which if a man leans, it will go into his hand and pierce it. So is Pharaoh king of Egypt to all who rely on him" (2 Kings 18:21).

It would appear that, at least to some degree, Hezekiah was counting on some help from a treaty with Egypt.

They next turn their attack indirectly toward God. If they had blatantly defamed the LORD right away the people may have risen to defend His name. Instead they put a question in their minds by saying, "But if you say to me, 'We trust in the LORD our God,' is it not He whose high places and whose altars Hezekiah has taken away" (2 Kings 18:22)?

This is a twisted and deceitful question for, if you remember, 14 years earlier Hezekiah had torn down the high places of the Baals and brought true temple worship back to Jerusalem. The high places weren't dedicated to God, but to the enemy and by tearing them down, Hezekiah was honoring the true God.

Fourteen years however is a very long time, and now the people may begin to wonder if Hezekiah had done the right thing or not. When we are going through hard times it is easy to think that God is mad at us or that we have done something wrong. It is hard to believe that maybe God has allowed this to bring us experientially closer to Him. The temptation is not yet enough to bring an open rebellion, but it does begin the process of doubt.

3. Brazen sarcasm

Now that the Israelites are shaken, the attack intensifies and the tone changes as they offer a sarcastic invitation. The Assyrians offer, "Now, therefore, come, make a bargain with my master the king of Assyria, and I will give you two thousand horses, if you are able on your part to set riders on them" (2 Kings 18:23). In other words, they are saying, "Obviously your attempt to withstand is futile. Even if we gave you 2000 horses you would still lose. In fact, you probably don't even have enough qualified men with the ability to ride a horse. You are fools to not give up right now."

Can you feel your stomach sink as you look out over this vast army and listen to what they are saying? Can you sense the spirits of Hezekiah's men melting? Can you hear yourself begin to believe the statements of the Assyrian army? "You know they're right. We can never overcome them. They're the Assyrians, who are we in comparison to them?"

This sarcasm is immediately followed up with a reprimand, as if they were little children, stating that even the best of their men shouldn't dare stand up to the least of the Assyrians. "How then can you repulse one official of the least of my master's servants, and rely on Egypt for chariots and for horsemen" (2 Kings, 18:24)?

4. Confusion

Now to add to the distress of the situation, the men of Assyria yell out, "Have I now come up without the Lord's approval against this place to destroy it? The LORD said to me, 'Go up against this land and destroy it'" (2 Kings 18:25).

These men from Assyria actually assert that it was Yahweh who sent them. (Notice that they are quoted as even using the proper name for God – LORD with all capital letters.) They are claiming that the God who made a personal covenant with Judah is the one who has sent Assyria to destroy them.

This is an obvious lie, but put yourself in their situation. If they are simply listening to their emotions in their circumstance, and only seeing what their physical eyes can see, it could easily appear that God is not on their side. They are totally surrounded and under siege. The Assyrians have annihilated everyone else who has crossed them and Judah has watched Israel when they were beaten and carried away into captivity. The natural mind might begin to believe that God is no longer on their side. "In fact", they might begin to think, "if God actually did send the Assyrians, it would be better to go along with them." The confusion continues and doubt grows.

5. Feeling isolated

It is now that we see another facet of the intimidation and pressure put upon Hezekiah. It has been alluded to all along, but now it becomes painfully obvious. Hezekiah is not the only one listening; all of Jerusalem is sitting on the walls and listening to the Assyrians. We know this because Hezekiah's dignitaries say, "Speak now to your servants in Aramaic, for we understand; and do not speak with us in Judean in the hearing of the people who are on the wall" (2 Kings 18:26). They knew that those on the wall were getting anxious and hoped that they could keep this discussion between themselves.

The Assyrians replied, "Has my master sent me only to your master and to you to speak these words, and not to the men who sit on the wall, doomed to eat their own dung and drink their own urine with you" (Isaiah 36:12)?

Making the threats public was part of the plan to put pressure on Hezekiah and the Assyrians knew that they were getting through. As a political leader, Hezekiah was on the spot and they wanted to turn up the heat. Hezekiah seemed to be all alone in this. Not only did he have to decide what to do, but he had to be thinking of what the people might be thinking. If they decided to rebel against him out of fear for their own lives, there would be nothing he could do. The Assyrians knew this. They knew that if their plan worked they could possibly sit back and allow a rebellion to win their battle for them. If the Assyrians couldn't sway Hezekiah, maybe they could use his own people to do it for them. If this happened, the whole Assyrian army could essentially be sitting in camp playing cards while Hezekiah's army destroyed itself out of fear.

6. Attack on God's ability

As the verbal assault progresses, the attack on the trustworthiness of Hezekiah and the character of God intensifies. The men of Assyria now make an all out verbal attack by yelling even louder and addressing the people of Jerusalem directly. They warn them neither to listen to Hezekiah nor to trust in God because, they claim, "He will not be able to deliver you from my hand" (2 Kings 18:29). By doing this, they not only undermine Hezekiah, but they assume authority over God Himself. The longer the people listen and take in what the Assyrians are saying, the more their faith is shaken.

7. Empty promises

Next, they do something very interesting. First of all, their tone seems to change. They begin to make promises to the Jews in the name of the king of Assyria by promising several things if the citizens of Jerusalem will make peace with him. The whole process echoes of some type of brain washing.

This is psychologically ingenious when you consider the circumstances. The people are shaken and afraid; they have been beaten by verbal abuse for quite some time now, and are growing more rattled and fatigued. They are feeling hopeless and can see no way out of their situation. In their weakened state they are vulnerable and looking for someone to rescue them, even if that rescuer is the very one who caused the hurt in the first place. The offer of comfort and the bold promises at this point in the attack could be quite appealing.

The citizens may have been thinking things like, "Maybe these Assyrians aren't really so bad. After all, they are giving us a chance to surrender in peace. It might be better to take a chance at trusting them rather than waiting for the alternative. Maybe what people say about them is all wrong and we should trust them."

At first glance what they promise may not seem noteworthy, until you look more deeply at the promises which are made. Several generations earlier, God had promised Israel wonderful things regarding the Promised Land which they were about to enter. By the time Hezekiah came around, they have already been living in the Promised Land for a considerably long time. From their vantage point, many of God's promises seem to be yet unfulfilled and they may have given up on ever seeing them, even though this lack of fulfillment is mostly due to their unbelief.

When we compare the account of what God promised to what the king of Assyria promised, they are amazingly close. Many years earlier Moses said,

> "For the LORD your God is bringing you into a good land, a land of brooks of water, of fountains and springs, flowing forth in

valleys and hills; a land of wheat and barley, of vines and fig trees and pomegranates, a land of olive oil and honey; a land where you shall eat food without scarcity, in which you shall not lack anything; a land whose stones are iron, and out of whose hills you can dig copper" (Deut. 8:7-9).

Now, all these years later, Sennacherib tells the people,

"Make your peace with me and come out to me, and eat each of his vine and each of his fig tree and drink each of the waters of his own cistern, until I come and take you away to a land like your own land, a land of grain and new wine, a land of bread and vineyards, a land of olive trees and honey, that you may live and not die" (2 Kings 18:31-32).

When compared with God's promises back in Deut. 8:7-9, the similarity is uncanny.

When we compare what God asked of His chosen people with what the self-proclaimed "great king" of Assyria asked of them, we find that they are identical. "Make your peace with me" (2 Kings 18:31). Or we could say, "Trust me" or "Submit totally to my authority and power." This king, who called himself the "great king", has now crossed the line completely and without any question. He has taken the place of God in his own mind. It is as if he said, "Your God cannot provide the things which He has promised, but I can. Trust me. Believe in me and I will provide for your every need and desire. The only thing it will cost you is your obedience and complete submission." Sennacherib, who had declared himself the great king, wanted Hezekiah and his people to place him in the position of God in their lives.

It is interesting to note that not only does Sennacherib use the proper name for God; he seems to know a great deal about God's promises. Again, Biblical history can shed some light on this topic. Years earlier, Jonah was sent to Nineveh to preach to the inhabitants there. He was to warn them of the coming judgment if they continued to reject God's ways. As we know from the story, the residents repented and there was a great revival in that city, but what you may not realize is that Nineveh was the capital city of Assyria.

What this means is that one of the forerunners to King Sennacherib had turned to the LORD, followed Him, and probably learned about His promises. By the time of Hezekiah, Nineveh had again turned away from God; however this spiritual heritage had been passed down in some degree – even if only as folklore. Either way, Sennacherib was not merely attacking the name of another nation's god; he was personally attacking YAHWEH – the God on whom he and his people had turned their backs.

8. All out attack on God

By now the Assyrians feel like they have set the stage by destroying the will of the people of Jerusalem. It is time for them to bring their final verbal assault.

The king of Assyria, through his servants, brings his attack to a grand finale by comparing the LORD God to the gods of all the other nations. He asks, "Who among all the gods of the lands have delivered their land from my hand, that the LORD (Yahweh) should deliver Jerusalem from my hand" (2 Kings 18:35)?

The people are shaken, afraid and confused. Their view of God has been challenged to the point of despair and all hope has been lost. As a believer, your final line of defense is God and His ability and desire to help you. If that is shaken, there is nothing left to lean on.

The Assyrians have come to Jerusalem in self-confident boldness and moved through a series of stages from indirectly attacking their faith in God's ability to claiming that their only hope was to trust in them as their god. This well thought out and much practiced attack had worked for them many times before and could be backed up, if necessary, with a devastating military force. Never in their lives was this particular group of people faced with such a decision. Do they trust their king and their God or do they bow to this foreign king?

The people's response

After all is said and done we see that the armor protecting the minds of the people of God still holds strong as we read, "But the people were silent and answered him not a word, for the king's commandment was, 'Do not answer him'" (2 Kings 19:36).

The fact that the people did not answer the attack is vital. First of all, it shows that Hezekiah still has control over his people and has not lost them completely. More importantly, it demonstrates that the people have not lost control of themselves.

The Assyrians probably expected the gates of the city to burst open and hoards of people to come flowing out to bow at their feet. However, when the only response was silence, they must have felt the tides begin to change. Their well developed plan of attack wasn't working, and for the first time in a long time, it seems as if Hezekiah has stolen the ball and is playing the game on his own terms. While he couldn't fight back or even refute their claims, one thing he could do is choose not to answer them.

The stage is now set for God to act on behalf of his people. However, like He so often does, God is waiting to act through one of His servants. Hezekiah now must make a choice; he can either respond to this threat with his own resources like he did before, or he can present himself as an instrument for God to use.

Comparison to our temptation

In these next few pages we are going to take another look at the stages that we just discussed. However, this time they will be applied to the temptations that we face on a daily basis. The enemy uses this same progression of psychological warfare with us as he brings temptation our way.

As a demonstration for this process I will use the temptation to worry as an example. This could be worry over a health issue, potential job loss, or relationship battle. Whether you are actually dealing with worry or some other temptation doesn't really matter, the process is often the same and God's answer still applies.

1. Boldness

When the servants of the self-proclaimed "great king" of Assyria came to Hezekiah, they came with great boldness and confidence in their ability to overcome him. Satan approaches us in the same manner and with the same unwavering air of confidence. It is important to remember that this boldness never backs down even when it is facing certain defeat. (Satan even mocked and tempted Jesus and had the audacity to ask Him to bow down at his feet and worship him.)

The goal of this type of warfare is to wear a person down with the aim of eventually winning him over. If someone believes his adversary is unbeatable, fear finds its way in and they begin to see the opponent as unbeatable. As this happens, the mind begins to shut down and the creative processes stop. Once a person believes he is defeated, he begins to act defeated and soon stops trying. This is the goal behind the "trash talk" before a prize fight or a street basketball game. Any fear instilled before the game becomes crippling during it.

Satan, like Sennacherib, has raised himself up to the position of the "great king" even though that position belongs to the LORD. It is very important for us to remember who is ultimately in charge. For, just as in Sennacherib's case, this ability to bully will only last as long as the LORD allows it. In the end, the victory belongs to the Lord and those who are on His team.

In regard to the temptation to worry, the attacks tend to come at our mind in the form of "facts" whether from the media, other people, or our own thoughts. Things like, "I know that someone is going to get laid off and I am the most disposable person here." Or these "facts" could possibly come from an article on the internet stating that this type of cancer is the most lethal that there is with only a small chance of survival.

Hezekiah too was in a situation with a sure outcome. Anyone who had been attacked by Sennacherib in the past had been either taken captive or killed.

2. Indirect attack on God

The next thing that we saw was an attempt on the part of the Assyrians to undermine Hezekiah's confidence by confronting both the physical and spiritual world of the Jews. They did this by questioning the choices that Hezekiah had made several years earlier and suggesting that God was not in those choices.

Satan's attack is similar on Christian's today. He will point out any physical weakness possible and use this to bring a seed of doubt. These weaknesses include our age, race, sex, physical impairments, the lack of talents and abilities or past failures. Anything that he can use to get our eyes off of God and on to ourselves will do the trick.

His attacks on our view of God at this point are just as subtle as they were in the early stages of Hezekiah's temptation. To outwardly challenge God and His love for us at this stage may actually push us into defending God's name and cause us to rise up against Satan's tactics. This stage is often accomplished through questions such as, "Has God really said…?" or "Are you sure that He made that promise to you? It was a long time ago. Maybe you came up with it yourself." If you are being tempted with the possibility of a layoff, you may be reminded of every mistake that you ever made while in this job. This will then serve as "proof" both to your impending layoff and to why God will not be gracious to you in this situation.

By doing this, he undermines our confidence in God and His promises to us. While this doesn't bring him total victory, it does shake the foundations of our faith.

Now, before you even realize that you are under attack, you may be overcome with the great power of your enemy and doubts begin to germinate in your mind as to the character of God. While these early doubts and fears are not all out rebellion on our part, they are the seeds that can grow into huge problems for us. They are sometimes so small that it is hard to even recognize them as temptations. Other times, they seem to be reasonable questions for us to consider as we evaluate our strength for what we are about to face. However, it is important to remember that it is not our strength that we are to rely on for this battle, but God's.

God's character and promises are our main weapon against our enemy; having doubts in regard to these is not a good way to walk into a battle.

3. Brazen sarcasm

This is the point when the source of the attack seems to move from somewhere out there to somewhere inside of us. As a person begins to embrace the lies of the enemy, they seem to become more personal and it feels as if the battle is within us rather than that we are battling someone else. It is like having a small metal sliver in your finger. At first, you can see what is causing the pain, but as it works its way down into your flesh, the sliver disappears from sight. Before you know it, you begin to think that there is something wrong with your finger rather than realizing that there is something in your finger that doesn't belong.

The voice of the temptation changes and what was once offensive to us begins to sound appealing. This means that rather than an external voice telling us to do something that we don't want to do, it begins to sound like our own voice, desires, and self-doubt that speak to us. Instead of saying, "You are such a loser," the thought in our mind morphs into, "I am such a loser".

This tactic changes your focus from your enemy to yourself and your own short comings. Fueling this attack are your own past hurts and negative views of yourself.

Once you are in this weakened state, the temptation now becomes more direct. The Assyrians offered to give the Jews 2,000 horses if they thought that they could put riders on them. In our personal temptations, Satan may slip thoughts in our mind like, "I know that I'm weak in this area and it is only a matter of time until I give in." Or he may give you thoughts that tell you everyone is making fun of you or that no one loves you. You may almost believe that you can read their minds and know that they are talking about you and what they are saying.

I began with an example of worry. In this situation you may begin to hear accusations regarding your right to even be in this position. You might start getting the thoughts that say, "I knew I would be found out eventually. I'm such a phony." Or, "Who am I to try to believe that God is going to change things just for me? I'm nobody special."

This is a very crucial time because the seeds of fear and doubt are now taking root and beginning to grow in your mind. Thinking on them and going over them in your mind is the fertilizer that gives them what they need to mature into full blown panic and misplaced fear. The more you dwell on these lies, the larger the enemy becomes in your mind and the more reverence you transfer from God, to your problem. As this continues, confusion takes over.

4. Confusion

Now that fear has given way to confusion, the mind is open for an all out lie. The Assyrians told Hezekiah that they were sent there by the LORD Himself to destroy them. Has Satan ever used this one on you? Maybe he has convinced you that the reason you are under such pressure is because God is punishing you for some past sin. It could be some large mistake that you made when you were younger, a moral failure in adulthood, or even something like not praying enough every day.

However, the Bible teaches us that Jesus was punished enough for all sin. As a Christian, you cannot be punished by God for your sins unless He somehow nullifies Jesus' payment - and this won't happen. We are, however, disciplined at times, and this leads to another lie that Satan uses frequently.

He blurs the very wide and distinct line between discipline and punishment. Punishment comes out of anger - discipline comes out of love. Punishment is given to pay for a wrong done - discipline is used to prevent future pain. Punishment tears down while discipline builds up. When a serial killer is convicted in court, society isn't overly concerned that he learns from his wrong, builds stronger character, and comes out of this a better person. They want him to pay for what he has done and keep him away from society. On the other hand, if your child cheats on a spelling test, you don't throw him in federal prison for 99 years to life. There will be consequences, but the goal is to show him a better way and give him the tools to become a better person in the long run.

God does discipline us for the things that we do wrong, and sometimes it can be quite painful. However, His discipline comes with a cleansing attribute rather than with condemnation. If Satan can get you to believe the lie that God doesn't like you or that you are anything less than the precious child that you are, then his battle is almost over. When someone has already been weakened by confusion about their own identity and God's character, then convincing them of this lie isn't a very difficult task.

Remember that Satan, just like Sennacherib, knows who YAHWEH is. In fact, Satan knows Him rather intimately. Satan formerly worshiped God and served as one of His Cherubim. He may even have been the one created to be in charge of the heavenly worship. When he was created, he was placed on the holy mountain of God and was in a special position of guarding the throne of God. In a discussion about Satan, God says, "You were the anointed cherub who covers, and I placed you there. You were on the holy mountain of God; you walked in the midst of the stones of fire" (Ezekiel 28:14). He knows God's promises to you and he knows how to twist them for his purposes, he even tried this with Jesus during his temptation in the wilderness. (Matthew 4:1-10).

His first assault on the human race was to bring doubt and confusion to Adam and Eve by questioning God's motives regarding His command not to eat from one particular tree in the garden. This seed of doubt grew into a seedling of mistrust and ultimately lead to all out rebellion. His methods haven't changed over time, and unfortunately neither has our gullibility to his deception.

5. Feeling Isolated

Since king, Hezekiah was the one responsible for making the right decision for his nation and their safety, their future rested on his shoulders alone. You may feel this same pressure in your circumstances.

Maybe the loss of an income or the threat of downsizing is filling your mind with worry for your future and the wellbeing of your family. Maybe cancer has returned, your teenage child is shutting down or your marriage is silently falling apart. It might be the temptation to get drunk while you are out of town on a business trip or look up some porn on your computer while you are home alone.

Whether it is something happening to you or something that you are tempted to do, one of Satan's goals is to make you feel alone in your struggle. People often don't want to ask for help because it makes them look weak in the eyes of others, and one thing that we often try to avoid is looking weak. We want to appear like we have everything all put together. We often convince ourselves that if we were given enough time, we would be able to work this problem out on our own. When this happens, you feel like you have been separated out from the herd and you have to fight Satan all on your own. This is a lie, and lies need to be fought with the truth.

The truth is that God has said, "I will never desert you, nor will I ever forsake you" (Hebrews 13:6). Not only are you not the only person who has been tempted in this particular way, but God Himself has promised to always be with you. Even though you feel completely alone and deserted by all others, the fact of the situation is that you are not alone and those feelings are based on the lies of the enemy. There is always hope when you are in covenant with the Almighty God.

6. Attack on God's Ability

While you have separated yourself from other believers and are hiding from God, your mind is open to attacks on God's ability to help you. Suppose you are the quarterback for the best team in the NFL and you are preparing for the Super Bowl. Now, let's say that the way that you decide to prepare is to watch films of your opponent's defensive line as they play their games throughout the regular season. You watch in horror as play after play they break through the offensive line and annihilate the quarterbacks. As the evening of watching progresses, you see quarterback after quarterback carried off of the field with broken limbs, concussions, and various other debilitating injuries. You barely sleep that night, and it is with clammy and shaking hands that you suit up on the day of the big game. Feeling alone and focusing on the enemy's strength has sapped all of your energy and will to play the game. You are now in an emotional condition that will bring clouded thinking, clumsy actions, and a broken spirit. If something doesn't change soon, the game will be lost without a fight.

It doesn't have to be this way, because in this story you have made one serious mistake. You are walking onto the field believing that you are alone and that the enemy is undefeatable. The fact is that you have left out one very important thing – your offensive linemen. Each one of these 350 pound piles of running muscle likes to do things like stop moving VW's as a warm-up for practice, and has never allowed any opposing team to get even one man past them.

With this line of protection at your command, the defensive linesmen are all but taken out of the game. You are now completely safe to do what your coach has called you to do.

As a Christian, you are not alone. In fact, you are in a covenant with the living God and no one, not even Satan, has ever been able to successfully oppose Him. Once you accepted Jesus as your savior, He bound Himself to you and promised to never leave nor forsake you. Simply knowing that you are never alone can free you up to play the game that has been set before you.

As a person in a covenant union with God, you are completely filled and surrounded with His love. Therefore, no matter how this particular situation works out, you are guaranteed to be taken care of. In fact, Romans 8:28 tells us that, "God causes all things to work together for good to those who love God."

7. Empty promises

However, we often find ourselves watching these videos the night before the big game and believing that we are facing the world on our own. The news threatens us with financial doomsday reports and tries to convince us that it isn't even safe to go out alone. Rumors at work bring fears of layoffs, aches and pains scream out impending diseases, and family and friends remind us of our weaknesses and past failures.

In times like these we tend to look to anything that will bring us relief. The enemy of our souls is more than willing to bring the promises that we desire. Drink this, eat that, buy something new, or leave your spouse and start fresh. On the other hand, the temptation may be to work harder, stay up later or think longer about the problem. All of these temptations come at a time when we are afraid and feeling alone. These things promise peace, love, and comfort; the very things that God has offered freely to us. Anything that Satan can promise to get our eyes off of God and on to something else will accomplish his goal.

The problem is that not only do these things leave us empty inside, but they offer yet another chance for him to bring shame and guilt into our lives. Only God can bring true and lasting fulfillment in our lives; any other substitute will leave us hungry and broken.

8. All out attack on God

Once we have allowed the temptation process to get to this point and we have accepted the empty promises of the enemy, it doesn't take much for us to believe all out lies about God. Things like, "If He really loved me He would not have let this happen," or "Maybe He speaks to some people, but not to me."

When you find yourself angry with God or distant from Him, it is time to look for the lie that you are believing about Him. Somewhere you have allowed the enemy to convince you that God is something less than He really is or that He feels less about you than He really does. As soon as you see the problem, you need to turn your back on the lies and turn your attention back to God.

"But the people were silent and answered him not a word, for the king's commandment was, 'Do not answer him'" (2 Kings 18:36).

Any human being who tries to fight temptation apart from God will fail, and will experience one of two outcomes. If you do fall into the sin, you experience the pangs of guilt and feelings of unworthiness. However, if you overcome the temptation and avoid committing that particular sin, but do it in your own strength, you feel pride in your ability to resist. Both outcomes fall under the realm of self-righteousness. On one hand the person couldn't make it work and on the other they could. Either way, they were doing it in their own strength.

Paul describes another kind of righteousness when he says,

"For not knowing about God's righteousness and seeking to establish their own, they did not subject themselves to the righteousness of God" (Romans 10:3).

As you can see from this verse, there are two kinds of righteousness talked about in the Bible; our righteousness and God's righteousness. The very best that you can do in your own strength – no matter how good it is – still can't meet up to God's righteousness. However, God never intended you to live up to His standards on your own; He desires to do it through you. You have to remember that only God can overcome Satan, and for this to happen in your life, you must trade your human strength for His strength.

Rest in God, resist the Devil, and God will fight for you. To rest in God is to let yourself experience His love and favor for you, His strength to protect you, and his ability and desire to care for you. You resist the Devil when you ignore his lies about you, your value, and God's desire to meet your needs. You will then see God's provision for you as you experience His love either directly or through the body of believers. Through the love of the body you can begin to see that you are not alone.

Hezekiah's Response

Try to imagine your response in Hezekiah's situation. You are a political ruler under physical attack; the minds of your people have been confused by the propaganda, and the longer you wait to respond, the worse the situation will become.

Putting someone under pressure is a good test of their character, and Hezekiah is no exception. His response was to tear his clothes and cover himself with sackcloth. Both of these actions were very appropriate things for a middle-easterner to do in times of great distress. It is what he did next that separates him from the crowd. He turned his back on the Assyrians, walked right past the people, and went directly to the house of the LORD. While this may have appeared like he was hiding from the problem, he was actually running to the answer.

It is important to remember that Hezekiah lived under the Old Covenant and at this time the Holy Spirit did not live in people as He does today. The immediate presence of God was in the temple where the Ark of the Covenant rested and was God's physical throne here on earth. For a Jew at that time to go to God, he would go into the temple. Hezekiah took his problem directly to the LORD, the One who had originally made a covenant with his ancestors and who had passed this same covenant down to him. He then sent messengers to Isaiah who was the mouthpiece of God at that time. Hezekiah realized that even though these threats were aimed at him, they were actually attacks on the LORD. He saw his physical problem from a spiritual perspective.

Through Isaiah, the LORD sent back a response to Hezekiah and all of Jerusalem. Even though Jerusalem was under attack, Isaiah acknowledged that the king of Assyria had actually taken up arms against God. God promised that He would put a spirit in the king of Assyria which would cause him to hear a rumor drawing him back to his own land. And just as God promised, this is what happened.

It would seem at this point in our story that all is well and Hezekiah has won without even lifting a sword. However, Hezekiah has yet another battle to fight and God has yet another time to prove Himself strong on Judah's behalf.

The king of Assyria did indeed leave to fight against another enemy, but his servants returned to Jerusalem with a message for Hezekiah. They said,

> "Do not let your God in whom you trust deceive you saying, 'Jerusalem shall not be given into the hand of the king of Assyria.' Behold, you have heard what the kings of Assyria have done to all the lands, destroying them completely. So will you be spared?" (2 Kings 19:10-11)

Imagine what went through Hezekiah's mind. It had seemed as though the time of fear was over and God had taken care of the king of Assyria. Had God failed? Had God changed His mind or was He angry with Hezekiah and therefore punishing Him?

Have you ever been through such a trial? You have fought in prayer, stretched your faith and finally, when it seemed that all was lost, you watched God come through. Thanking God for His love and faithfulness, you call your friends or share your testimony in front of church. Then, maybe the next day or week, the doubts returned; the job fell through, the cancer came back, your loved one changed his or her mind.

The temptations to give up during these times may be even stronger than the first time around. You may not feel like you have the strength to go through the struggle all over again. But, it is not time to give up. It is time to settle in and watch for God's strength to be unleashed in your favor. The greater the attack, the greater the victory.

It is at this moment that Hezekiah makes a decision to "set his mind on things above" (Colossians 3:2). He reads the letter brought by the servants of the king of Assyria - knowing fully the implications of refusing to surrender - and makes his decision. Hezekiah again enters the presence of the LORD and prays one of the most beautiful and pivotal prayers in the Bible.

> O LORD, the God of Israel, who are enthroned above the cherubim, You are the God, You alone, of all the kingdoms of the earth. You have made heaven and earth. Incline Your ear, O LORD, and hear; open Your eyes, O LORD, and see; and listen to the words of Sennacherib, which he has sent to reproach the living God. Truly, O LORD, the kings of Assyria have devastated the nations and their lands and have cast their gods into the fire, for they were not gods but the work of men's hands, wood and stone. So they have destroyed them. Now, O LORD, our God, I pray, deliver us from his hand that all the

kingdoms of the earth may know that You alone O LORD, are God." (2 Kings 19:15-19)

This particular crisis drew Hezekiah back into prayer – a prayer that won an unwinnable battle. Hezekiah knew that though his enemy was physical, his answer would be found in a spiritual battle. Even today, in our modern world, the same principle holds true.

Section 2

Hezekiah's Prayer

Chapter 7

In this section we will be looking at Hezekiah's prayer in 2 Kings 19:14-19 and following the four steps which he took as he stood before the LORD.

Step One: Go Directly to God

"Then Hezekiah took the letter from the hand of the messengers and read it, and he went up to the house of the LORD and spread it out before the LORD" (2 Kings 19:14). Before consulting advisors, before checking the opinion polls and before fear had any more time to set in, Hezekiah went into the presence of the LORD.

It is important to point out once again his position. He was around 35 years old and the ruler of a nation. The country was in a national red alert and he was the one on whose shoulders rested the sole responsibility for their safety. It was his decision as to how to respond to this letter from the king of Assyria. His future and the future of his people depended on the decisions that he would make in the next few minutes. It is safe to assume that there was intense pressure on him, both from within himself and from others, to make a speedy decision. Yet, in the face of that pressure, he chose to retreat into the presence of the LORD.

What he did when he got there is a wonderfully picturesque example for us to follow. He literally took the letter and, "spread it out before the LORD." He opened the letter and placed it before God as if to give Him an opportunity to read it for Himself. Hezekiah physically laid his burdens down on the altar.

When you are faced with trials and temptations, when the enemy's attacks are continually pounding on your door, when it seems as though God has forgotten you and all is lost, go into the presence of the LORD. This may mean that you step foreword for prayer at the altar or that you sit alone in your living room and bring your mind to rest.

Once you mentally enter into the presence of the LORD, lay your "letter" before Him. One way that you can do this is to list on paper the concerns that you have or those things that bring you the most fear or shame. After you do this, physically lay them down in front of you as you tell God all about your situation. Take your time as you do this. Knowing that God already knows everything, we often simply ask Him to help us with "our problems." Why go over everything with Him when He is fully aware of the situation?

The fact is that we need to hear it. We need to list all of our fears and allow the emotions that are attached to them to surface. We need to be honest with ourselves and with God about how big and frightening this problem really is to us. While this may seem to bring more fear than you are comfortable with, that fear will be absorbed throughout this process.

At this point you have not asked God for anything, you have simply laid your letter before Him. When this time is over, burn or tear up the paper to signify that you are leaving these problems and concerns there with the LORD. Remember that He is the Almighty God who loves you more than you can possibly comprehend, and the One who has all things and situations in His hands.

This will take more than 10 or 15 minutes because you need to give yourself time to really feel what is going on. If you haven't done this before or if your letter includes several things, it may be something that you work on over a few days. Make this list as complete as possible and be as emotionally honest as you can because this will make the process that much more freeing.

Step Two: Remember Who God Is

After placing the letter on the altar, Hezekiah prayed, "O LORD, the God of Israel, who are enthroned above the cherubim, You are the God, You alone, of all the kingdoms of the earth. You have made heaven and earth" (2 Kings 19:15).

Why did he start out this way? Does God need to be reminded about who He is? Is this kind of an address to make sure that Hezekiah is talking to the right God? Or, does Hezekiah pray this way to get God's favor - to butter Him up - so that he can get what he wants? Obviously this is not what he is doing, but these words are far more than simply beginning his prayer by saying, "Dear God."

Hezekiah is actually reminding *himself* of who God is. By doing this, he is combating the fear and uncertainty in his own mind by recalling the vastness of God and His position of complete and unchallenged authority. The situation which he faces is very real to him: the siege, the reputation of the Assyrians, the torture to him and his people, what would appear to be certain destruction… Hezekiah has learned the vital Biblical principle that tells you to, "Set your mind on things above." He is choosing what he will believe. Though his options are simple, Sennacherib or God, the choice is very difficult. Hezekiah removes himself from the situation, gets alone with God, and then sets his mind on truth.

The situations that you face may not seem as urgent or as threatening as what Hezekiah faced, but they are just as real, and to you, they are just as big and just as threatening. In the same way that the Assyrians were taunting Hezekiah, the enemy has been whispering in your ear with the intent of setting your mind on how powerful and terrible your situation is. If Satan can get you to concentrate on the problem at hand, you could spend your time fighting an enemy that you can't beat without ever taking the time to pray.

> Remember that, "Our struggle is not against flesh and blood, but against the rulers, against the powers, against the world forces of this darkness, against the spiritual forces of wickedness in the heavenly places." Eph. 6:12

In the New Testament, Paul tells you to, "Set your mind on things above, not on the things that are on the earth. For you have died and your life is hidden with Christ in God" (Colossians 3:2-3). Choosing to think on what is true is not some sort of magical formula which will make it happen. Faith is not a method that we use to control the universe, but rather something that flows from a mind which is focused on truth.

There is an example in the New Testament of Peter and John reminding themselves of who God is in Acts chapter 3 and 4. They were teaching the people out in the open when the priests and temple guard took them into custody and put them in jail over night. The next day before they were released they were warned never to speak of Jesus again, "Or else."

When they got back to the other believers they prayed a prayer that is recorded in Acts 4:24-30. They were praying during a very critical time in their lives. Their prayer was pivotal. They begin by saying, "O Lord, it is You who made the heaven and the earth and the sea, and all that is in them" (Acts 4:24).

Notice how they approached God the same way that Hezekiah did. They reminded themselves of God's power and authority; not only in their lives, but His authority in the entire universe. In fact, their prayer lasts for seven verses; the first five verses talk about God and what He has done, the next verse asks Him to "take note of their threats," and the final verse goes back to talking about God.

Again, even in the face of persecution from those who had just killed Jesus, the disciples focused on God and His ability more than on their need. By placing their attention on Him, they were able to put their minds at rest and approach their prayer session with the proper perspective; God is God, we're His kids, and no one can change that. Since He is all-powerful and He loves us more than anything else, we can rest in His love and ability.

Jesus said, "If you abide in My word, then you are truly disciples of Mine; and you shall know the truth, and the truth shall make you free" (John 8:31-32). Freedom doesn't come from struggling against temptation or from battling our enemies with all of the human strength and willpower that we can muster up.

Freedom comes from knowing (not just intellectually - but intimately) the truth. God is God whether you acknowledge it or not, but when you choose to believe all that is true about Him and how it relates to you, you can personalize this truth. You can then look to God and call Him, "my God."

This may be the most important step in the process. Don't shortcut here. Make sure that you take as much time as you need to bring yourself back to a point of faith in an all-powerful God who loves you more than life itself. Continue to work through your memories of the times that He saved you and took care of you in the past – other times when it seemed that all was lost. Remember all of the stories in the Bible that demonstrate His love and concern for His people. Don't leave this place until the Holy Spirit has breathed a new fire in your soul, for this fire will carry you through your fight of faith.

Christians often pray that God would increase their faith. The problem with this prayer is that "faith" becomes a greater focus than the God in whom that faith rests. Let's say that you need to drive from New York to California and you own a 1973 pickup that has bald tires and an oil leak. You would not have much faith in your vehicle or your chances of making it to your destination. What if you repeated to yourself over and over, "My truck can make it, my truck can make it?" No matter how many times you said it, deep down you would still be anxious about the trip. However, what if you had to make this same trip but were given a brand new Rolls Royce to drive? Suddenly, you would have more than enough faith in your vehicle. In fact, you would probably be looking forward to a nice long journey in your new car. Whether or not you would need to buy extra oil would not even cross your mind.

Many Christians see God like that 1973 rusty pickup. Whether they believe that He can't meet their needs, is too busy to meet their needs, or just doesn't want to meet their needs, it all amounts to the same thing. They don't have much faith that their needs will get met, and no amount of faith building will help. The problem isn't their faith; it is their view of God. The fact is, our God is a Rolls Royce in a world of rusty cars. If you want to increase your faith you need a more comprehensive view of God. Not only does He have the entire universe at His disposal, but He loves you dearly and would give His very life for you. The more that you see God in this way, the more faith you will have without even trying hard to believe.

Again, don't leave this place until this fact is securely etched in your soul. God honors a prayer of faith, and your view of God is where your faith comes from. Take as much time as is necessary to build up your view of God and revel in His view of you. It may feel like you are putting off praying for the need at hand, but you are actually cleaning your lens so that you can pray boldly and with accuracy.

Step Three: Ask

After Hezekiah deliberately separates himself from distractions and enters the presence of the LORD, and after he reminds himself of the character and abilities of this God who has made a covenant with him, he then brings his petition to the LORD. Sometimes our prayers flow more from our fears of what might or might not happen than they do from our faith in God. However, prayers that bubble up from a spirit that is secure in the love and power of God move forth to change the world. You are the same person in either situation; your personal power hasn't changed. All that has shifted is the focus of your fear.

It is, however, important to remember that God knows our weakness and works in spite of them. In Romans 8:26, Paul tells us that, "the Spirit Himself intercedes for us with groaning too deep for words." Sometimes our needs are so overwhelming that we don't even have the words to pray, but even in these times we can depend on His strength and love for us.

In this instance, "fear" means whatever you honor or respect. Any reasonable adult has a well placed fear of fire. This doesn't mean that you are afraid to look at, talk about, or be near fire, it simply means that you wouldn't pick up a burning coal and put it in your pocket. Having a fear of fire allows you to appreciate its benefits while also appreciating its power. In the first scenario above, the fear is of the situation and therefore you are honoring, respecting and giving homage to that situation. However, in the second example, the fear has been rightfully placed in God. To "fear the Lord" is to give Him a place of honor and respect in your life.

Hezekiah notes that the words spoken by the Assyrians are not against him, but against God. He prays, "Incline Your ear, O LORD, and hear; open Your eyes, O LORD, and see; and listen to the words of Sennacherib, which he has sent to reproach the living God" (2 Kings 19:16). In this he takes the battle off of his own shoulders and puts it onto God's shoulders where it belongs.

He is honest with God as he presents his need. He is not using positive confessions or flowery statements as he presents this need. He says, "Truly, O LORD, the kings of Assyria have devastated the nations and their lands and have cast their gods into the fire, for they were not gods but the work of men's hands, wood and stone" (2 Kings 19:17-18).

Hezekiah is in a covenant with God and he knows what this means; his problems are God's problems and God has promised to take care of him. To be in a covenant is to be in a very tight relationship. It says in part, "Whatever is mine is yours and your enemies have now become my enemies. I will be loyal to you at all costs and will defend your life even if it costs my own." While it would be helpful to be involved in this kind of a relationship with another human being, consider what it means when you are in a covenant with God. All of His resources, all of His power, and all of His riches are there for you when you need them. With this on your side, you could go into any battle, no matter the circumstance, and know beyond a doubt that you will come out victorious.

How does this apply to us? If you have asked Jesus into your heart, you are also in a covenant with this same God that fought for Hezekiah. He has promised that His resources are now your resources, His strength is now your strength and His very life is now your life. After you have adjusted your perspective about God and your situation, you can, "draw near with confidence to the throne of grace, that (you) may receive mercy and may find grace to help in the time of need" (Hebrews 4:16).

Sometimes prayers are spoken frantically or from a position of begging, or maybe even begrudgingly as a duty. Following Hezekiah's example can prepare a person so that his prayer can come from security, confidence and love. The prayer of faith isn't one that comes from pumping ourselves up in our ability to believe really, really hard. It is simply a prayer that comes from a position of faith. Faith comes from a true understanding of who we are and who God is, therefore, to increase your faith, you simply need to deepen your understanding of God.

First, go to God and get alone with Him in a way that you can focus on Him and Him alone. Second, take some time to remind yourself of who God is and recount in your mind everything that He has done for you. If you are concerned with a financial problem, for example, remind yourself of that time when you didn't have enough for groceries and someone brought over some food, or when your paycheck came late and instead of bouncing checks you realized that there was $100 more in the account than you thought. If you don't have any personal experiences to draw from, look to the Bible and recall that the One with whom you are in covenant owns "the cattle on a thousand hills" (Psalm 50:10) and has promised to "never leave you or forsake you" (Hebrews 13:5). God cannot lie, and every promise that He has made to you in the Bible is a promise based on His character and bound by His love for you.

If you can find no example of God's faithfulness in a situation similar to yours then prepare yourself to see the hand of the Almighty in a way you have never seen before. Remember, His name is "I AM" and He wants to reveal Himself to you as being all that you need in this situation.

Bask in the warmth and beauty of God's love for you. Realize His unlimited power and resources to back up His promises. Then move on to step three and ask of Him whatever you need. Your emotions may still be high and you may still feel uncertain, but emotions don't affect the truth. Ask boldly and confidently, just as a little child asks for a sandwich or another cookie. Your Daddy loves you and is fully prepared to take care of you.

It almost seems as if Hezekiah went to God as a child would go to his daddy to tell him that a bully was picking on him. Not only was the bully threatening Hezekiah, however, he had the nerve to say that his Daddy was a wimp who could not protect him even if He tried. You can almost feel the LORD standing up from out of His throne, lifting his little boy into His loving arms, and going out to set the record straight.

Step Four: God's Honor Alone

Hezekiah asked God to deliver them, "that all the kingdoms of the earth may know that You alone, O LORD, are God" (2 Kings 19:19). We can see Hezekiah's love for his God as he ended his prayer, for even in this time of great and immediate need, Hezekiah was more concerned about God's honor than his own safety. Let the goal of your petitions be to further the glory and honor of God's name.

"Delight yourself in the LORD and He will give you the desires of your heart" (Psalm 37:4). As you delight in God, as you abide in Him, as you fill your mind with Him, your desires will come into line with His desires for you. As this happens, He will grant you whatever you wish because it harmonizes with what He wishes for you, and what He wishes is always good.

God's goal for us is to work all things together for the purpose of transforming us into the image of Jesus (Romans 8:28-29). With this in mind, we can look for His hand in every aspect of our lives and allow Him to renew our desires and prayers.

YOUR OWN PRAYER

I'd like to encourage you now to take some time to write out your own prayer. Review the steps below and work through them to fit your particular situation.

While praying silently in your mind is a perfectly acceptable method of prayer, writing it out in a journal or on a computer can really help you to focus your thoughts. Find a place where you can be uninterrupted for a good length of time and go before God. Lay out your struggles, fears, or concerns before Him. Write out your praises of Him as you remind yourself who He is and the many wonderful things that He has done in your life and the lives of others. Then, while you are experiencing the peace that comes from sitting in His presence, ask Him to meet your needs.

As you pray, you may discover that you are hearing from Him more than talking to Him. You may discover that He has guidance for you and that your final "asking" might end up differently than you originally intended. Write down whatever you hear Him saying to you. Hold on to this and look back at it often as a way to check its validity and to encourage yourself.

Step One: Go directly to God

Begin by picturing yourself in God's immediate presence receiving His full, undivided attention. He has set all of His other tasks aside so that He can meet with you right now.

Pray something similar to the following:
"God, I'm here because I know that You love me and are interested in my needs. Please use this time that I have set aside to come before Your throne to accomplish all that You have intended. Thank You for meeting with me here and I ask that You would change me during this meeting. Open my eyes to see You more clearly and to appreciate all that You are and all that You have done for me."

Write out your own prayer…

Now, lay your own "letter" out before Him. In other words, write out what is troubling you, in detail, and lay it down before you. Picture yourself in God's holy temple, kneeling at His alter, and place your letter on that alter for Him to read.

This isn't a time to be strong or stoic with your emotions. This is a time to be real with God and yourself. Acknowledge the fear. Accept the feelings of hopelessness. Allow yourself to experience the overwhelming emotions that you have been hiding inside.

This is important for two reasons. First of all, God already knows how you feel and how weak you really are – He won't be surprised by your smallness. Secondly, the more deeply that you embrace where you already are, the more deeply you will be able to surrender these feelings and beliefs to God when the time comes. While facing the depth of your fears and weaknesses is difficult, it is a necessary step in surrendering yourself into God's love.

Step Two: Remind yourself who God is

Remember the importance of this particular step. The goal is to fill your mind with the greatness of God and His ability to meet you in your need before you ever present that need to Him.

Begin by choosing something (nature, children, rain storms, the ocean, etc…) and telling God how wonderful He is for creating it.

Pray something like this:
"Lord, I am thankful for the amazing beauty and intricacy of Your creation. I know that You work in every small detail by sustaining and

renewing life. From the smallest bacteria to the vast reaches of space, You are fully in control…"

Continuing with this thought process, write out your own prayer in your journal…

Stay here as long as necessary and come back as often as you need to during the rest of this process. As you absorb yourself into God's presence and glory, the fears and hopelessness that you acknowledged in step one will diffuse into God's endless love for you.

While a teaspoon of arsenic may be deadly on its own, if it is dissolved into a universe full of pure water, it is quickly rendered ineffective. Your worries, fears, and anxieties are real, and can be as deadly as arsenic. However, when they are dispersed into the limitless ocean of God's pure and unending love for you, they begin to fade away. God is real and His life-giving love for you is real. Therefore, when you are in His presence and experiencing that love, you are living in the "real world". To "pray without ceasing" is to learn to live your life in this reality.

Step Three: Ask

Now is the time to remember that you are in a blood covenant with Almighty God. He is the "Living God" and the "Ancient of days." He has vowed by His own name to love and protect you with nothing less than His very own life.

In Hebrews 13:5 God is quoted as saying, "I will never desert you, nor will I ever forsake you." This is an amazing verse when taken at face value in English, but when you look at the words in the original Greek, this promise comes alive.

The word "never" is made up of two words. One of them could be translated to mean, "God forbid that it ever come into existence." And the other word has the job of giving whichever word it is with the meaning of the absolute negative. God is essentially saying, "I will never, ever, in a million years desert you. In fact, the thought of it should not even be allowed to come into existence."

The word "desert" is also interesting. It means, "to relax, loosen, to not uphold, or to let sink." That last one really speaks to me. I have never been able to master the art of swimming. In fact, when my wife tried to teach me to swim early on in our relationship, we found out that when I kicked my feet, I actually went backward. Add to that the fact that I don't seem to float very well, and you can understand that I am not overly comfortable in deep water.

When I meditate on this verse, I picture myself in the deep, dark waters of life resting calmly on God's almighty hands. He, Himself has promised to never allow me to sink.

With that in mind, pray something like this: "LORD, You have chosen to make a covenant with me, and in that, have placed all of Your resources into my account. I am totally safe in Your hands and completely surrounded by Your love. Today I need…"

Write out your own prayer asking God boldly as His child who is deeply loved.

Step Four: For God's Honor Alone

This final step allows us to again focus on God and His sovereignty. He is the beginning and end of all things and He acts according to His glory and perfect will. Begin this step by listing the ways that the changes in your situation, attitudes, and expectations will positively affect the people in your areas of influence. Next, commit to watching for opportunities that will allow God to flow through you to bring positive changes to their lives. The answer to your prayer doesn't end with getting what you asked for. The ultimate goals for God's actions are not only to love you, but also to draw others to His love and grace.

For your final step to this process, pray something like this:

"Father, as You meet this need, I ask that You keep my mind focused on You and Your provision rather than on my own abilities. I thank You that when this has been accomplished, others will be able to see You more clearly in my life and will be drawn to You. I thank You that this will give me a new chance to tell them of Your goodness. Specifically, ..."

Continue in your journal with your own prayer.

Remember that prayer is a chance for us to get to know God on a more intimate level and an opportunity for us to surrender our will and desires to Him.

GOD'S ANSWER TO HEZEKIAH

It appears that God waited to act until Hezekiah prayed. God told Hezekiah, "Because you have prayed to Me about Sennacherib king of Assyria, I have heard you" (2 Kings 19:20). God knew Hezekiah's need before Hezekiah asked, but He chose to wait until Hezekiah asked before He did anything. We may wonder why He waited so long and allowed Sennacherib to get away with as much as he did. One possible explanation for this lies in God's desire for us to truly know Him.

If God would have never allowed Sennacherib to even come against Jerusalem this would have spared them a great deal of trouble and worry. However, it would also have prevented them from learning a great and wonderful lesson about God's provision. It would have taken away their opportunity to learn more about God's name.

A person may know full well that God has the power to heal, but once they are sick and they cry out to God and He heals them, they really "know" Him as their healer. He moves from the God who heals people to "God *my* healer". Someone who has lost a job and now faces an uncertain future may have heard of God as a provider or giver of peace, but during those long painful nights something happens and God becomes Jehovah Shalom – "God *my* peace". A new name for God and a new aspect of His character is revealed. Jesus promised, "In this world you have tribulation, but take courage; I have overcome the world" (John 16:33). Allow God to take your hand and lead you into His path of overcoming.

Christians may fall into the belief that says, "If God really loved me, He would fix this problem for me." God's goal however is not to take away all of the bad things that come across our path. His desire is to teach us to rely on Him and to live in union with Him as we work through our struggles.

113

God was totally in control of this situation between Hezekiah and Sennacherib from before the foundation of the earth. In His response to Hezekiah's prayer, God said to Sennacherib, "Have you not heard? Long ago I did it; from ancient times I planned it. Now I have brought it to pass, that you should turn fortified cities into ruinous heaps" (2 Kings 19:25). Although Sennacherib was feeling very powerful, God explained that the only reason he was able to defeat the other cities is because God made their inhabitants "short of strength." He allowed Sennacherib to defeat them as part of His plan. Rather than being the "great king" that he claimed to be, Sennacherib was actually operating in forced servitude to the true Great King.

After the LORD has carried Hezekiah into the presence of the bully, He gave him a ring side seat so that he could watch as God protected His honor. The LORD continued with Sennacherib by telling him that He knew what has been going on. He even knew when Sennacherib sat down or stood up, He knew when Sennacherib came in or went out, not one word or action has passed by the LORD unnoticed. (2 Kings 19:27-28). All this time it had seemed that God was absent or unconcerned, but in reality He was simply waiting for the perfect time to act. We even find out that He set the whole thing up to accomplish His own goals - there are no surprise attacks against God!

How often do we stand in fear of our enemy with the belief that God has forgotten us, only to find out that He was simply waiting for the perfect time to act?

Not only is God perfect, He is deliberate and unwavering when it comes to showing His love for us.

His punishment for Sennacherib is the same thing which Sennacherib threatened to do to Hezekiah. God told him that He would put a hook in Sennacherib's nose and a bridle in his lips and would drag him back to Assyria. As Hezekiah watched, God did to the bully the very thing that he threatened to do to Hezekiah.

That night, without Hezekiah or his army even having to leave the walls of Jerusalem, God sent His angel into the camp of the Assyrians. That one angel killed 185,000 of Sennacherib's men in just one night, and the next day Sennacherib went home in shame. Just like that, God spoke and the battle ended. All of the worry and fret accomplished nothing, but one word from the mouth of God ended the threat of Sennacherib forever.

Later, when Sennacherib was worshipping his false god, two of his own sons killed him. The one who called himself "the king, the great king of Assyria" was only a man and no match for the God of Heaven and those who call on His name.

The enemy of your soul is no different. He was kicked out of heaven for trying to place himself in the position of the "great king" when he and one third of the angles rebelled against God. God, however, quickly crushed the rebellion and expelled His

115

enemies from His throne room. Now, when these enemies surround you and threaten to place you under siege, you can turn to the same God that stood up for Hezekiah.

Conclusion

This is the account of the King of a Middle Eastern nation who lived several thousand years ago, and yet the struggle is as contemporary as the challenges that we face today. God has promised that He is the same "yesterday, today and forever." Our struggles and temptations really haven't changed over the centuries. The comforting thing is that neither has our God. He still loves us and desires to prove Himself strong on our behalf.

Take a good long look at your "enemies," whether they are physical, emotional or spiritual. Then, turn your back on them, lay them out before God and look into His eyes of love. Allow Him to become for you what you need today.

If you have never asked Jesus to forgive your sins and come into your heart, then you are what the Bible refers to as spiritually dead. What a dead person needs more than anything else is *life*. Jesus said that He is the LIFE. Present yourself to Him today. Ask Him to take all that you have (your emptiness, loneliness, fear and pain) and replace it with His LIFE. Allow Him to fill you and begin to unfold His plan for you.

Once the life of God lives within you, you are His child and God takes great offense to anyone who dares to mess with His kids. When the enemy taunts you, remember that there is only one Great King, and He is your dad and your friend.

117

About the Author

Jon Hoeraut (hair-off) is a teacher and freelance writer. He has an MA in counseling and has worked in the past with individuals and families, along with spending several years counseling children in a residential setting.

Jon and his wife, Lynn, live in Farwell, MI.

Livin' Free is a Christ-centered ministry that teaches *the reality of our identity in Christ along with the freedom that this new life brings*. In John 8:31-32 Jesus says, "If you abide in My word, then you are truly disciples of Mine; and you will know the truth, and the truth will make you free." Jon's goal is to teach the truth about Jesus in a clear and experiential way that will help Christians find the freedom that God offers to each of His children.

To schedule Jon or Lynn for a speaking engagement, or to find out more about available teaching materials, email Jon at jon@livnfree.com.

Livin' Free
www.livnfree.com

Made in the USA
Charleston, SC
22 February 2013